I0049757

Acclaim for
Maximizing Customer Loyalty

"*Maximizing Customer Loyalty* offers globally valid and actionable thoughts to reshape an organization to focus on the importance of customer loyalty. The distinguished guidance by C.W. Crutcher includes insights on the acceleration of customer service excellence. The book is a must to keep up with the momentum of competition by presenting ways to promote customer loyalty."
—**Özgür Dinçer, Group Head of Internal Audit & Business Excellence, Pegasus Airlines, Istanbul, Turkey**

"Bill Crutcher masterfully illustrates actionable and accessible customer service strategies and tactics! A required resource for any professional who desires to create exceptional customer experiences."
—**N.J. Robinson, President, Hi-Tech Leadership**

"*Maximizing Customer Loyalty* has been a great addition to our business communication course curriculum. Customer service is the heart of any organization. The content is robust and speaks to many service careers. If you are ready to elevate your students or team, we highly recommend investing in education and development opportunities with the National Customer Service Association. They're an amazing business partner!"
—**Samantha Dowdy, Director of Workforce Development, The Excel Center—Goodwill**

"With Bill Crutcher's permission I can share that I had the privilege of serving him under the most strenuous of circumstances and was always impressed with his ability to see the bright side of every situation—even the indomitable one he was in at that point. His positive attitude is transmitted through his newest book, *Maximizing Customer Loyalty*. For a guide

on how to have comfortable interactions in even the most difficult of circumstances, I recommend you read, absorb, and use the information in this book."
—Uday Popat, M.D., Professor and Hematologist in the Department of Stem Cell Transplantation, Division of Cancer Medicine, University of Texas MD Anderson Cancer Center, Houston, TX

"When you work with Bill, he guides you and your team to a higher level of performance and personal satisfaction, and you appreciate his straightforward yet respectful approach to making needed change easier to understand and absorb. This book offers the same guidance in an easy-to-understand format that can serve as a quick reference for specific issues or a global tool to reset your organization's customer service philosophy.

"In this decade of social awareness, one bad Trip Advisor post or one-star Yelp review can seriously damage your business. You best have a great way to improve your customer service, assuring that your organization stays in business and grows. Use *Maximizing Customer Loyalty* as your ready reference tool. You will not be disappointed. Better customer service goes a long way in the hearts of your team members and grows loyalty to your company.

"I wish you all much success."
—Steffan Block, Landlord of The Wheatsheaf Inn, Corston Bath, England

"Bill Crutcher has authored the definitive book on customer service. There are practical, easy-to-apply examples and quizzes at the end of each chapter to ensure the reader gets a hands-on experience. The easy-to-read, no-nonsense approach makes this book perfect for applying the principles in a post-pandemic business world. For readers who want to take their customer service skills to the next level, this book will pave the way."
—Rick Sainte, Entrepreneur and Multi-Million-Dollar Sales Producer, Murfreesboro, TN

"As a professional mentor and coach in the areas of leadership, personal development, and strategic planning, I look for expert resources to further my knowledge and provide to my customers for their use. As a leader of global customer service in previous years, Bill's knowledge and passion for service is valuable for any individual or organization interested in rising to service excellence! This book includes straightforward, easy-to-apply, and useful guidelines that can individually or collectively be put to immediate use. You won't be disappointed."

—C.J. Privoznik, Founder, Principal of STW Solutions, Inc.

The Ultimate Guide to Delivering Incredible
Frontline Customer Service

Maximizing
CUSTOMER
LOYALTY

C. William Crutcher

Foreword by
Erin Blecha-Ward, President & Founder
Evolved Experience Solutions, Inc.
Former Head of Fan Experience, Atlanta Hawks

DIAMIN PUBLISHING

Maximizing Customer Loyalty: The Ultimate Guide to Delivering Incredible Frontline Customer Service

Copyright © 2022 by C. William Crutcher

All rights reserved. No part of this book may be reproduced or used in any manner without written permission of the copyright owner except for the use of quotations in a book review.

Published by DIAMIN Publishing

Cover and interior design by Pam Germer, quadegraphiqs.com
Editing by Nivi Nagiel, finalcopy.biz

All images copyright by the author or have been licensed by the author, unless otherwise noted.

Although the author and publisher have taken every precaution in the preparation of this book, the author and publisher do not assume and hereby disclaim any liability to any party for any loss, damage, or disruption caused by errors or omissions, or resulting from the use of the information contained herein.

1. BUSINESS & ECONOMICS / Customer Relations.
2. BUSINESS & ECONOMICS / Skills. 3. BUSINESS & ECONOMICS / Training

ISBN 979-8-9865075-0-7 (Paperback)
ISBN 979-8-9865075-1-4 (Ebook)

First edition 2022

For

Diane, Amie, Mindie, Autumn & Carson

&

every professional on the front line of customer service

Contents

Foreword

Customer service, in modern times, has become a novelty for many businesses. Rather than providing consistently exceptional service, they allow their standards to slip to the point where many guests are genuinely surprised when they do encounter great service. The irony, as poignantly illustrated in this book, is that customers are the reason we have jobs in the first place, and servicing them should be central to all we do, never an afterthought or an inconvenience.

Having spent nearly two decades in the entertainment, sports and service industries, I've seen firsthand how sports brands (in particular) that take their guests for granted when their team is performing well pay the price with empty stands when team performance slips. Conversely, those who maintain consistently high experience standards, regardless of wins or losses on the court, find that fans come back year after year because they love the game-day experience, not just because they are jumping on the bandwagon. This concept extends to all industries, and in many ways is even more critical because that inherent "fandom" is much more fleeting for necessity brands (grocery stores, retail, restaurants, etc.), and there is always a competitor ready to take the business.

Ninety-five percent of guests who have a negative brand experience will either tell others in their life, exit the brand or both (Zendesk), but only 1 in 26 will tell you, unless you have a process in place to understand guests' needs and make it easy for them to engage with you for support (CXM). During my time heading up fan experience departments for minor league, college and professional sports teams, I realized that to provide a consistently excellent experience (the type detailed in both of Bill Crutcher's books), we needed a way to hear from fans in real time, so we could respond quickly and effectively. In 2018 I launched Evolved Experience Solutions, Inc., to bridge that gap. I now have the privilege of providing a real-time analytics platform to frontline managers and team members in the sports, entertainment, hospitality, dining and hotel industries to empower them with technology to provide the level of service Bill details throughout this book.

As Bill so eloquently outlines, service is a mindset, one that is not fleeting but has to stem from a true desire to help and care for others. I use the term "Memory Maker." We are all in our own industry, yes, but collectively, we are transforming brand moments into unforgettable memories for guests. While heading up Fan Experience for the Atlanta Hawks, I was tasked with overhauling the employee engagement training and recognition for the more than 1,200 full– and part-time staff members. One of the challenges was that, for years, team members had been given tasks to complete in their shifts, not a bigger purpose. We implemented S.M.I.L.E. as a core cultural pillar (S=Southern Hospitality, M=Make a Moment, I=Individuals Matter, L=Loyalty, E=Empower). We introduced the training through a series of small, two-hour sessions where staff from all departments workshopped together in groups of six to build connections and learn about the culture. I remember one of the more challenging sessions had about 15 percent of the group comprised of Atlanta police officers. They were very vocal that they didn't want to be there or take part. That said, they did, and about a week later, two officers approached me at a Hawks game and said, "Listen, we need to talk with you. This guest was lost and we helped her find her seat and had the mascot go visit her and her son. We definitely made an S (Southern Hospitality), M (Make a Moment) and I (Individuals Matter)." It was amazing! They took what we taught them and not only brought it to life, but were EXCITED to share. That happened all across our team; every department, from concessions to security to parking, started to embrace the idea that THEY were part of the guest experience, not just the players on the court. They weren't just ticket takers; they were hosts. Not just security, but protectors. It may sound like a small change, but it's actually quite monumental. When you don't feel your role is more than a "job," it's hard to get excited, motivated and put your best foot forward each day. Seeing the impact you have beyond and sharing a language that indicates the huge importance of every role on the team makes work fun, valuable and engaging.

You don't have to be a leader to make that change happen. I did a lot of managing up to get organizational buy-in from the top down. If you're in a role that doesn't feel fulfilling, raise your hand and suggest ways to enhance the frontline experience. Now, more than ever, retaining those incredible employees should be a top priority for businesses. If you find your voice isn't valued, I promise you there are other organizations that would love your talents and passion. But hopefully, your leaders see your ideas as a spark to transform moments into memories for you and the guests.

So as you look at the service you deliver, focus not just on process, but on execution, and be fully committed to consistently providing exceptional service and curating unforgettable experiences. The memories you help create will stick with guests far longer, and have a far greater impact on your bottom line than you may realize. Bill's knowledge, passion and experience in this space provide an easy-to-follow, high-impact guide for cultivating this service mindset and delivering a personalized approach to each guest you serve.

Remember, *"Building a good customer experience does not happen by accident; it happens by design"* (Clare Muscutt). I hope you find this resource valuable in designing an excellent service culture for your brand.

Erin Blecha-Ward
President & Founder
Evolved Experience Solutions, Inc.
Former Head of Fan Experience & Entertainment,
Atlanta Hawks & Stanford University Athletics

Introduction

Every day in the United States, millions of customers are served by millions of direct-contact Customer Service Professionals. These service professionals interact with their customers in a variety of ways: in-person, by telephone, text, email or virtually. Some channels of interaction are understandably more challenging than others.

When customers are physically in your presence, you receive important communication cues that allow you to be more effective in your dealings with them. Other communication mediums lack some, or even many, of these face-to-face cues, and thus make it more challenging to successfully serve your customers. These cues can include facial expressions, body language (nonverbals) or vocal intonation. And while the absence of these communication cues may create additional challenges for positively interacting with customers, you must always find a way to provide the best customer service experience possible.

This book is designed to significantly enhance the skills of ALL frontline Customer Service Professionals and to support you in delivering exceptional customer service experiences. Whether you work in a bank, a hospital, a call center, an online fulfillment warehouse, or one of the thousands of other industries, if you are the direct link—point of contact—to your organization's customers, then this book is directed to you. And this book applies to anyone providing service of any kind to customers—whether they are internal or external to the organization. Use this book as a reference guide to customer service—referring to it regularly.

As you work your way through this book, consider these wise words, attributed to the great Greek philosopher Aristotle:

"We are what we repeatedly do. Excellence, therefore, is not an act but a habit."

As a direct-contact Customer Service Professional, you must think in terms of how your customer interactions contribute to greater customer loyalty and do so consistently—day in and day out. Because you—the frontline Customer Service Professional—have a monumental impact on overall customer loyalty to your organization. So do your work every day as though your job depends on it, as does every other employee's job in the organization. Because they do.

CHAPTER 1

Foundations of Customer Service

Attitude of Service

At the root of successful customer service is our attitude toward serving others. Do you genuinely enjoy doing so, or is it more like the saying, "Come to work on Monday, looking forward to Friday!"? Extremely effective Customer Service Professionals truly enjoy serving others and do so enthusiastically.

So, what is "attitude"? Simply defined, attitude is **the way we think and feel about someone or something.** It is part of our "private" selves—unknown by those around us—until we engage in behaviors that reflect our attitudes. Let's take a look at a couple of real-life examples that reflect the impact of attitude on outcomes.

1. Several times during my life, I decided, for various reasons, I needed to lose some weight. My clothes were too tight; I became a bit winded when involved in physical activity, and overall did not like my appearance. So, during these "health-focused" times, I ate more nutritiously and focused on exercise, which allowed me to successfully lose 20–30 pounds—every time. Unfortunately, after some time had passed at the lower weight, I started eating "wrong" foods again and avoided exercise. Not surprisingly, it didn't take long to return to my previous weight, which really didn't bother me until the next time I felt the need to get healthy.

2. While serving in the Army, I picked up the nasty habit of smoking cigarettes. At that time, many of us in the military as well as the general public smoked. Unfortunately, at that time, the negative long-term effects of smoking weren't as widely known or shared. After I was out

of the military and learned more about the harmful effects of smoking, I wanted to quit. (It didn't hurt to have my personal physician living next door to coach me!) So, many years ago, I had my last cigarette at 8 a.m. on a Thanksgiving Day. (Yes, you remember these kinds of details because of the significance such a drastic change plays in your life.) And the best part is, I have never taken even a single puff since that day. I was quite impressed with how much better I felt after quitting and was proud of my stamina and determination to do so.

What was the difference between my recurring, but temporary, weight-loss periods and my successfully stopping smoking for good? It was my **attitude.** With weight loss, I never developed an authentic attitude about the long-term value of healthy eating and exercise. If I had, not only would I have engaged in a healthier lifestyle, but I would have done so automatically every day. Essentially, this healthy lifestyle would have run on autopilot. But instead, I just manipulated my behaviors long enough to get the weight-loss results—albeit temporary—I was seeking.

With smoking, I was able to alter my attitude by understanding and embracing the harmful effects of smoking on me, my family and friends. And because my attitude toward smoking authentically changed, I have had no desire to resume the habit whatsoever. In summary, I manipulated my behaviors regarding weight loss and failed, but with smoking I created an "autopilot" that allowed me to subconsciously refrain from smoking.

From a customer service perspective, individuals with a positive attitude toward serving others are typically much more effective in their jobs. And the best news is, like me and my smoking, a positive attitude can be acquired and sustained for your personal and professional victories!

Our attitudes—which guide our behaviors—are formed from a number of sources, which we will explore in more depth in the next chapter, "Insight into Customer Behaviors."

The Role of the Customer

Several years ago, I was facilitating a day-long Teaming workshop for an upscale restaurant. The management team selected a day they were closed so that all staff could participate. We were in an upstairs banquet room that had several windows overlooking the restaurant's entrance.

We were discussing the importance of customers, but I wasn't getting much feedback, so I asked all the participants to gather at the windows looking down at the main entrance. I then asked them to imagine that was a day they would be open—and not a single person was lined up to enter the restaurant. What would this mean to their business? Needless to say, the conversation became active and animated. The employees began sharing the negative consequences of having no customers. They ended this exercise with a much stronger appreciation of the people who walk through their front door, as well as how to care for and serve them so they want to return and spread the word. They also realized that it takes the whole team to produce high quality and consistently excellent products and services.

Without customers, you do not have an enterprise. Obvious as this may seem, we don't always focus on providing excellence in customer service. The reality is that customers are the reason you are in business. Yes, various people may benefit from your business, including you, other employees, stockholders and the community at large, but the primary and most essential people to your business are your bill-paying customers. Without their current and, hopefully, repeat business, your organization has little sustainability and no lasting purpose for existence. Making the customer your number one priority is crucial to your business's ongoing success.

The bottom line is that businesses exist because of their customers. The wise businessperson knows that the customer makes tomorrow possible and behaves accordingly every day, providing service excellence, which leads to customer loyalty.

The Root of Service: Attitude, Knowledge and Empowerment

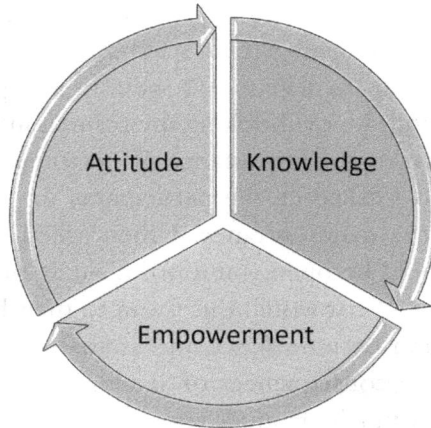

Excellence in customer service relies on key precursory conditions. The first of these is an **attitude of service.** True Customer Service Professionals understand that to effectively serve, they must put their own wants and needs behind those of the customer. That is not to say that the customer wins and the company loses, but rather that the customer's needs and issues are addressed, not to the detriment of the company, but satisfactorily for all parties.

Let's imagine a well-attended sporting event has just ended, and everyone is trying to exit the parking lot as quickly as possible. Chaos ensues as everyone struggles to be the next one out, cutting off others in the process. Now imagine everyone adopting a "you first, then me" attitude. The picture is calmer and the lot empties more quickly. People leave less stressed. It is the same with effective customer service. When you employ a "you first, then me" approach to serving, you become a better listener, act more cordially and create relationships that lead to long-term customer loyalty. You create constant "win-wins."

Recently, a colleague and I went for a late lunch at a local chain restaurant. As we approached the register to place our order, the employee was focused on her cell phone. My colleague cleared his throat to get her attention. She looked up and let out an exaggerated sigh—her way of letting us know she did

4

not appreciate being interrupted. The notion of an attitude of service was clearly not in her vocabulary, let alone her customer interactions. She was displaying a "me first and then you, when I get around to it" attitude. We shared our experience with the manager and then left without ordering. A business's survival depends on customers taking the time to provide constructive input, and management listening and seriously considering it. As an aside, we all have an obligation to be a good customer with the businesses we patronize as well.

The second root of service excellence is **knowledge**—knowing your job and knowing it well. Know your products and services and what they can do for the customer. While any job involves a learning curve, customers are never impressed with "I don't know" or "I'll have to check" as your standard response. It is incumbent on you, as the Customer Service Professional, to thoroughly understand your job. Also important is understanding how your job fits with others in the organization. Whether you are assisting with a bank deposit, providing a specialized report or performing online technical support, your customers rely on you to be the subject matter expert. When you answer the phone or stand behind the counter, customers assume you are there to serve them and have the needed knowledge and attitude to do so. Don't disappoint them, as you may not get another chance.

Have you ever been to a restaurant where your server appeared to not know their menu? While we should certainly appreciate that learning a job takes some time, it becomes frustrating when the server responds to every inquiry with the disappointing "Let me check." Servers should take the time to learn what's on the menu and what substitutions or modifications can be made. And to serve with a confident, friendly attitude. Lacking knowledge about your products or services does not instill confidence in your customers. This, in turn, directly impacts their loyalty to your business.

The third root of service excellence is **empowerment**—the authority or power given to someone to do something. It permits the Customer Service Professional to serve their customers more efficiently. Dealing with employees who are not able to resolve service issues as they occur is frustrating for customers. It is essential that as the Customer Service Professional, you know what latitude you have to serve your customers. When there is a service breakdown, do you have to "check with the boss" or are you able to offer alternatives to satisfy the customer?

How good do you feel as a customer when an employee offers you some acceptable alternative, on the spot, when a service breakdown occurs? You quickly appreciate that the business values its customers.

Naturally, some organizations allow their employees greater autonomy than others. If appropriate empowerment is lacking and employees regularly need permission before acting, the service professional may want to share potential empowerment strategies with leadership for their consideration. Appropriately placed empowerment has the opportunity to greatly impact customer loyalty, and as a Customer Service Professional, you will grow in your skills, which enhances further career opportunities for you.

Who Are Your Customers?

Simply defined,

> **A customer is *any* person or group to whom you provide a good or service.**

6

Typically, when we think of a customer, we think of a person or group outside our organization. You likely view those who pay the bills—external customers—as your only real customers. Often disregarded as a customer is the person who works down the hall from you or in another department or building in your company. Your suppliers, delivery people, volunteers— all are your customers as well. A well-known customer service quotation, attributed to several people, states:

> **If you're not directly serving the bill-paying customer—**
> **then you'd better be serving someone who is!**

The intent of the quote is to emphasize that, as an employee, you had better be serving someone who benefits your business. Otherwise, your job isn't needed and neither are you!

Every employee of every organization has customers, whether external or internal to the organization, or both. If a person does not create something that is or could be used by another—whether immediately or in the future—then why would that job exist? The report generated by the finance department, the supplies ordered by the office clerk and the restrooms cleaned by the custodian all contribute to the marketable outputs of the organization. While some jobs may be more directly linked to the external customer, every job is important to ultimately serve the bill-paying customer and effectively retain that customer-focused competitive advantage. Working together is the only way to make this happen.

VIEW OF CUSTOMERS

Ultimately, how you think about your customers determines how you serve them. When you think of an individual or group as a **"user"** of your work output, you tend to believe that your obligation is complete when the product or service has been delivered. So, when you deliver your monthly finance report to the operations department, you have no other responsibility to them until next month. You communicate little with the "user" between monthly reports. This thinking leads to doing much less for the operations department than might be valuable for them.

When you think of an individual or group as a **"customer,"** you behave much differently toward them, as you view your obligation to the "customer" as never really complete. You interact more regularly to ensure the product or service you are delivering effectively meets their needs. If not, you can modify your deliverables to maximize their value to your customer and thus increase the overall value of your services to the end customer. You meet with your customer, exploring how you can be of further assistance; you communicate what schedules you must follow, any updates to the schedules and the flexibility you have to better serve them. You also share how they can be a better customer—what they can do for you that will help you support them more effectively and efficiently. Remember, the customer you are serving may be internal or external to your organization, an "end" bill-paying customer or a partner who delivers supplies or works beside you. Every customer is vital to your organization.

So, while viewing the external bill-paying customer as your sole customer may seem intuitive, you must recognize the vital importance of your internal customers as well. Adopting this broadened perspective of customers enhances your interactions and deliverables and results in a more successful organization, from which you directly benefit.

Misconceptions of Customer Service

Most of us are familiar with common pronouncements regarding customer service such as "the customer is always right." While these statements contain elements of truth, in general, they cannot be practically implemented business strategies.

Let's explore some of these key misconceptions and discover their impactful realities.

MISCONCEPTION #1: Customers are an Interruption

The reality is that customers are **NEVER** an interruption. They are the reason your business exists. Without them, your organization serves no purpose.

Let's look at an example. Imagine you are attempting to accomplish a certain task and just need a little more time to finish. Then, lo and behold, in comes a customer. What bad timing for you. Do you think at that moment your attitude may be unconsciously projected and felt by the customer? Words, vocal tone or nonverbals are highly likely to expose your true feelings.

Please remember that customers are NEVER an interruption. Let me say this again: **bill-paying customers are never an interruption!** They not only pay your salary but they drive improvement and innovation. Think about the many products that exist today because of input from customers. It is their feedback—if we wisely listen and use it—that allows businesses to adjust products and services and how they are delivered. Look at Coca-Cola's Freestyle soft drink dispenser. Customers kept demanding more drink options, and this machine now delivers over one hundred soft drink flavors—each one personally selected by the customer.

Allow yourself to be gratefully "interrupted" by your customers and you may be surprised by the positive consequences. You may pleasantly discover the growth opportunities your customers provide. The bottom line is that customers make your organization's tomorrow possible.

MISCONCEPTION #2: Customers Have to Do Business With You

In reality, there are **always** options available to your external customers, and even some of your internal customers. Some employees may think their job is free from competition and, therefore, enjoy a false sense of job security. Examples could include employees of the accounts payable department in a private business or the street department crew of a municipality. For their direct customers, there may not currently be an alternative source for those services. In reality, though, these functions could always be provided by a third-party vendor. If you think your job could never be outsourced, you are quite mistaken. Some entity "out there" would love to take on your work functions and will not hesitate to lobby your leadership for the opportunity.

In one of my former corporate roles, we were regularly approached by outsourcers—businesses that wanted to do the work our employees were doing. They would always promise better service at costs lower than ours. This possibility was not lost on our employees. One day, an employee told me she heard that part or all of her department might be outsourced. Though it was just an unfounded rumor, she was concerned about losing her job. What was my coaching? I told her to do her job the best she could. And by doing so, she raised the bar for any outside entity hoping to replace her and diminished the likelihood of our services being outsourced. Make yourself invaluable to your organization and your customers!

To ensure your employer would never consider outsourcing your job, do what you do, to the very best of your ability. You must treat your customers consistently, so they **WANT** to do business with you, not because they **HAVE** to. Coming to work every day and believing that a competitor wants your customers should cause you to enhance your customer service—because it is absolutely true!

MISCONCEPTION #3: Products and Services Alone Create Customer Loyalty

The reality is that long-term loyalty is directly impacted by the strength of your ongoing relationship with the customer. For years, many businesses focused on a single business line. For example, if you needed a refrigerator or dishwasher, you went to an appliance store. Now, many companies offer multiple product lines—often under the same roof. We can purchase a refrigerator, dog food and vitamins all from a single store. Competition for multiple products seems to exist at every intersection and is continually growing.

Since customers can readily select from many vendors for the same product, businesses must now focus on differentiating themselves by the level of service they provide. Customer Service Professionals embrace this focus and understand the critical need to build loyal relationships with all customers by consistently enhancing services.

External customers may initially select a business because of its products, prices, proximity and associated features. However, research indicates that prices are often not the primary consideration once the customer has a **positive relationship** with employees of a particular business. How many people, for example, question the prices of a hair stylist or barber they have patronized for a long time? Positive relationships have been established with these providers. Both customers and providers appreciate one another and the ongoing positive interactions. The same is true for virtual service providers. While online service may not feel as personal, customers still develop a relationship with the business and decide daily whether to continue it based on how we feel we were treated, the quality of products received, timely delivery and good communication, among other factors.

MISCONCEPTION #4: Customers Will Remain Loyal Over Time

In reality, customers are **NOT** yours for a lifetime. They may only be loyal to you or your organization through the VERY NEXT INTERACTION! It takes a lifetime to create that coveted customer loyalty, and yet it can take just one service breakdown to lose that customer, forever.

Sadly, when a customer leaves, they rarely share their reason for leaving directly with the business. They will, though, more often than not, share their inadequate experience with their friends and colleagues, perhaps even exaggerating the circumstance as they become entranced telling the story. This is not the type of publicity that any organization desires. It is, therefore, incumbent on the Customer Service Professional to maintain the kind of relationships that will weather an occasional breakdown—because they will happen from time to time. Remember—opportunities to create customer loyalty are never lost. Someone will take the ones you miss.

MISCONCEPTION #5: Your Service Is Compared Only to Others in Similar Industries

The reality is that your strongest competition is **ANYONE** who raises a customer's service expectations—ANYONE! For example, let us assume a customer has just taken their car to a quick-oil-change shop. The employees at the shop were exceptionally courteous, worked quickly and then explained what they did in easy-to-understand terms. The customer leaves the oil-change shop with a smile on their face because of this incredibly positive experience.

Now, assume that customer then comes to your business. Their barometer of customer satisfaction is not the comparison to how they were last treated at your business or at one of your competitors', but rather at the oil-change facility. The customer will now be reflecting on their most recent customer service experience and either consciously or subconsciously comparing your business accordingly. Your job is to constantly raise the service bar for the next business your customer patronizes. As a business, you are competing with every other business, whether in-person, virtual or other interactive means. You must "up your game" with every interaction.

MISCONCEPTION #6: To Your Customers, You Represent Just a Tiny Portion of the Company

In reality, to your customers, you **ARE** the company, regardless of your specific job duties. If you are communicating with them—regardless of medium—the customer expects that you serve their every need, and speak on behalf of your company. Even in businesses with thousands of employees, the one dealing with a customer will be the one person (to them) who defines care, quality and attitude for your entire company.

As an example, a service technician for a telephone company is handling a service outage in a small rural town. While checking the lines, he is stopped by an elderly gentleman who shows him his telephone bill. The customer says he is confused by all the line items on the bill—taxes, fees, etc. Instead of saying to the gentleman, "Billing is not my job; you will have to contact the business office," the service technician says, "I will

12

have someone from our billing department call you to explain the bill's details." While the customer is happy—for the moment—it is critical to follow through to make sure promises are kept. The service technician should call the main office requesting that someone from billing contact the customer regarding billing questions. That is an "attitude of service" in action. To the customer, the service technician WAS the company, and his actions left a positive image of it.

The following quotation, attributed to automaker Henry Ford, provides an excellent summation of your role as a direct-contact service professional:

> *"To the world, you may just be one person.*
> *To one person, you just may be the world."*

MISCONCEPTION #7: The Customer is Always Right

While this axiom has existed for many decades, the reality is that the customer is not, in fact, always right. However, as the direct-contact Customer Service Professional, your focus is not to prove to the customer how they are wrong. While alternative approaches may be part of the end discussion, at earlier stages of the conversation, the customer's error does not matter. Starting the conversation by proving the customer wrong is a perfect recipe for a service disaster.

When the customer's point of view or actions are incorrect, it is important to share with them that you understand the complexities they are dealing with. Your job going forward is to help fix the "wrong" and clarify how both of you can agree how to proceed in the future to avoid another similar circumstance. Phrases such as "I'm sorry, we may not have been clear . . ." or "I can see how this could be a bit confusing . . ." are important to continuing the conversation to a mutual satisfactory end.

The most important focus must be on moving forward, identifying and implementing a solution to the current issue and establishing clarity on how to avoid such a situation in the future. Do not lay blame—not on the customer and not on the company and definitely not on another department or co-worker—it just stalls the resolution. A simple statement such as "Why don't we try this" will likely be well received by the customer and shift the focus from the current breakdown to a mutually acceptable solution.

It is equally important to set the stage for future interactions, while equipping the customer with more accurate steps going forward to assure this situation is not repeated. You may end with "The next time we do this, we should try . . ." which will leave the customer with a more positive feeling for the next interaction with your business.

Remember, being **appropriate** is exceedingly more important than being **right.** The successful Customer Service Professional knows that laying blame does nothing to enhance positive long-term relationships. In the end, the goal is to leave each customer interaction so that they want to remain your customer.

Customer Wants vs. Needs

Simply defined:
- To **"want"** is to have a desire to possess or do something.
- To **"need"** is to require something because it is essential or very important.

These definitions seem straightforward and are, until we begin to implement them personally. Then the lines blur almost unconsciously. We find ourselves saying "need" when what we really mean is that we want something. We might also subjugate our needs and put them off to wants and, therefore, deem them unnecessary right now and maybe ever. We all face this conundrum every day, repeatedly, and we typically don't even realize it or its impact on us.

So how do these often-misinterpreted terms affect your customer service world? While customers will tell you what they want, you must decipher their real needs and then help them understand and support the recommendations. It has been said that if Henry Ford gave customers what they wanted instead of what they needed, he would have invested in faster horses. Thus, it is important to recognize and remember what customers both want and need.

In summary, what do customers actually *need?*
- Quality products and services
- Options—recognizing this is not a one-size-fits-all world
- Clear and timely communication
- Positive, supportive relationships with business points of contact
- Understanding of their particular situation
- Reliable partnership—one that can be counted on in every interaction, every time

While customers may say they want specific products or services, their actual wants can be expressed in the following statement:

Customers want their needs met to their satisfaction, not yours or the business's; on their timetable, not yours; while being treated fairly and respectfully.

In summary, a mastery of these foundations of customer service—knowing and living them every day—is essential to the long-term success of **ANY** business. It is important to fully appreciate the value of your customers—not just in the revenue they provide today—but the promise they hold for your business tomorrow and beyond.

Chapter Review Questions

1. The three root elements of service include:
   a. Attitude, purpose and knowledge
   b. Attitude, knowledge and empowerment
   c. Preparation, communication and approach
   d. Knowledge, abilities and character

2. If you manipulate your customer service behaviors without adjusting the underlying attitudes, you can always expect long-term customer satisfaction and loyalty.
   a. True
   b. False

3. Which of the following is a customer?
   a. A visitor asking you for directions
   b. A guest in your hotel
   c. An employee in another department of your company who receives your customer service contact reports
   d. A person attending a concert
   e. All of the above

4. Thinking of internal customers as "users" allows us to more effectively serve them.
   a. True
   b. False

5. There are often positive consequences to being "interrupted" by a customer.
   a. True
   b. False

6. When you feel your organization has a monopoly on what you provide your customers:
   a. Acquiring customer feedback on your products or services is not critical.
   b. You can consider limiting direct customer interaction times.
   c. Job security is really not an issue for you or your employees.
   d. Your job functions may be more easily assumed by a third-party vendor.

7. Which of the following is not necessary for maintaining customer loyalty?
   a. Waiting for your customers to contact you before following up with them
   b. Keeping your promises
   c. Maintaining a positive, can-do approach
   d. Treating customers uniquely

8. Once customers become loyal to you or your organization, they are naturally your customers for a lifetime.
   a. True
   b. False

9. To your customers, you are the company, regardless of your actual job duties.
   a. True
   b. False

10. It is not correct to believe that the customer is always right; therefore, when the customer is actually wrong, you should:
    a. Let the customer know why they were in error.
    b. Advise the customer you are a subject-matter expert regarding this situation.
    c. Tell the customer to never try that same approach in the future.
    d. Focus on moving forward with a solution and not laying blame.

11. A "want" is requiring something because it is essential or very important.
    a. True
    b. False

12. Which of the following do customers not need?
    a. Clear and timely communication
    b. The lowest prices for products and services
    c. Positive, supportive relationships with business points of contact
    d. Understanding of their particular situation

13. Which of the following is true?
    a. Great products and services are all that is required for customer loyalty.
    b. The customer service I provide may be compared to the service received in a completely different industry.
    c. Your customers do not expect you to speak on behalf of the entire company.
    d. It is sometimes acceptable to ignore a customer.

14. Poor customer service is often more readily tolerated if your company's prices are quite low compared to others.
    a. True
    b. False

15. Wants vs. needs—what do your customers actually need?
    a. Clear and timely communication
    b. Appreciation of their particular situation
    c. Effective partnership
    d. Positive, supportive relationships with business points of contact
    e. All of the above

CHAPTER 2

Building Customer Relationships

As we discussed in Chapter 1, sincere and ever-evolving relationships are the cornerstone of long-term **customer loyalty.** Let's take a moment to expand on the positive consequences of productive relationships for the Customer Service Professional.

Impacts of Positive Relationships

You support others. When you have exceptionally good relationships with your customers, you are in a better position to satisfactorily serve them. Think about a positive relationship you have with another person. The reason you have that relationship is that you have learned a great deal about that person and appreciate their attitudes and behaviors. You are able to have more candid conversations (while always respectful) and understand one another well. As you build and maintain these relationships, you gain more insights into the customers' wants and needs—enabling you to more effectively serve them. Over time you earn their respect and trust—and they yours—which can positively influence their buying decisions to the benefit of your business.

You advocate. When you have the kinds of insights into customers that are necessary for a lasting relationship, you are equipped to support and promote their needs within the organization. Your company may for example be considering a change in a service or product offering that you feel might negatively impact your customers. With your relational knowledge of your customers, you are able to share this impact with your organization's leadership and contribute to an outcome more beneficial for all.

You help yourself. There are several dimensions to how positive relationships can help you, the Customer Service Professional.

- **Synergy.** Synergy is the increased effectiveness that results when two or more people work together. With customers as your "partners," you can enjoy much more success and satisfaction in your daily work efforts.

- **Sharing the pain/gain.** Relationship partners can collectively experience outcomes that are positive as well as those that are constructive. Sharing an experience with a colleague, for instance, is an opportunity to grow, and to get input on how the situation might have been handled differently or to receive a compliment on how well you handled the interaction. Another benefit of relationships is the respect and trust both partners enjoy—both the joys of accomplishments and the shared pain when we fall short.

- **More fun.** Simply stated, collaborating with others and accomplishing goals as a partnership is just more enjoyable.

- **Recognition.** It feels good when your customers appreciate what you do for them and acknowledge your contributions, particularly to your work colleagues and leadership, as well as to the customer's peers, who may become customers themselves because of the recommendation from a satisfied friend.

21

You minimize error impact. Because you have worked so hard to create and maintain positive customer relationships, errors that may occur because of a flawed process or human oversight (yours or someone else's) are often accepted as a rare event. They are overlooked by your customer or brought to your attention politely yet constructively. Obviously, it is incumbent on you and others in your organization to explore the cause of the error and correct it appropriately, keeping the customer in the communication loop to raise their satisfaction even more.

You create more referrals. Who can better sell your organization's products and services than a highly satisfied customer? By consistently treating your customers fairly and respectfully and delivering on your commitments punctually, they will tell others. With today's social media options, their opinions can influence a wide audience. And these customers, your biggest fans, become your organization's valued promoters.

Influencing Relationships

To better understand how these highly coveted positive customer relationships are built, let's first explore why customers **leave** businesses—regardless of our best efforts.

According to Michael LeBoeuf's book *How to Win Customers and Keep Them for Life,* customers leave for the following reasons:

- 3% moved and the business was no longer easily accessible (for businesses that require face-to-face interactions such as dry cleaners, restaurants and healthcare).
- 5% developed other relationships that attracted the customer's business.
- 9% left for competitive reasons; the customer found better products or services with another provider.
- 14% were dissatisfied with the product or service.

- 68% left because of an attitude of indifference toward the customer by the owner, manager or other employee. This is worth repeating: 68% left because of an attitude of indifference toward the customer by the owner, manager or other employee!

This should be an eye-opener: **Most customers left because of how they were treated—primarily by a single individual in the organization!** Obviously, these employees did not possess or act with an attitude of service. Businesses spend an estimated six to seven times more to acquire a new customer than to retain a current one. These statistics suggest that a vast improvement in customer retention efforts, including regular employee training, is absolutely critical to overall business success.

Research further suggests that the sources of customer dissatisfaction include the following:

- **An unfulfilled promise.** It is critically important that you only make the promises you can keep and then make sure you keep the promises you have made.

- **Rude or inefficient service.** Rudeness and inefficiency have no place in your business if you want to stay in business! Treat every customer as though you want them to return—because you do! They are the reason you are in business and they can choose to go elsewhere —"voting with their feet"—never to return.

- **Conflicting messages from different employees.** It is important that all customer-contact employees understand the organization's procedures and communicate them consistently to customers. Hearing one thing from Employee A and another (conflicting) assertion from Employee B is frustrating for customers.

In one of my corporate jobs, I traveled frequently. Twenty-four hours before departure, we could call the airline for a complimentary upgrade to first class based on availability. This became a bit of a game. If the agent indicated there was no upgrade space available, we would hang up and then call right back. We always got a different agent, and in many cases, there would magically be upgrade space available. It was clear that some agents did not understand the procedure, or worse, chose not to be bothered processing the upgrade. Either way, this inconsistency did not leave a positive image of their training or their commitment to the customer.

- **The feeling of being taken advantage of.** You may be an expert in your field, but remember, your customer probably isn't.

Imagine you are driving on the highway and your car is vibrating excessively at higher speeds. You take the car to a service center for diagnostics and repair. The service technician says you have a blown front passenger strut, and the repair will be $495. He further states that while they do that repair, they will rotate and balance your tires at no charge. Is this a good deal? You probably don't know. It could be that all you really needed was your tires balanced to eliminate the vibration. Or possibly you did have a bad strut.

Because we are not subject matter experts in most fields, it is incumbent upon the service professional to take time to explain their products and services to the customer and answer all questions in understandable terms. If you already have a positive relationship with this vendor, you will likely believe their diagnosis and repair plan. This is yet another benefit of establishing relationships that are built to last. And remember, if customers ever have cause to question your honesty or integrity, they will soon become **former** customers, and will likely take those they influence—either current or potential customers—with them.

- **Delays and long waits to receive products or services.** If you anticipate that a product is going to be backordered, tell your customer up front. If your restaurant has an unexpectedly higher number of diners one evening and you haven't staffed accordingly, share that there may be a slight delay in food delivery. You might offer a complimentary drink or appetizer to show appreciation for the customer's patience. Bottom line: It is extremely important to manage customer expectations honestly and promptly.

- **Defective or inferior products or services—unfulfilled expectations.** A guarantee doesn't mean that a product won't break or that all promises will be fulfilled precisely as stated—no matter how hard a company may try. The key is how you manage the breakdown with the customer. What are you doing to minimize the impact on them? Do you deliver that replacement lawn mower or offer a complimentary meal? Things will go wrong. How you recover matters.

- **Lack of communication—not knowing what is happening and thus thinking the worst.** In another travel situation several years ago, our airplane pushed back from the gate at a major international airport, and we sat on the taxiway for three exceptionally long hours. During that time, we received not a single update from the cockpit. To say that the passengers were upset would be putting it mildly. The key for any business is that when there are unforeseen delays, provide regular updates to your customers.

- **Dishonesty—also known as "business suicide."** This one is extremely simple to handle. Tell the truth, even if it may not be what the customer wants to hear. Lying is the highest form of disrespect, and in certain situations could result in legal consequences.

Customer Service Professionals understand that customers can and do leave businesses for various reasons. The role of the service professional, and the business overall, is to take positive steps to prevent or at least minimize reasons for leaving.

Relationship-Building Practices

How does the Customer Service Professional create those treasured positive relationships? As we indicated earlier, while you cannot prevent all customers from leaving your organization, you can take positive steps to build relationships that lead to overall customer attraction and retention.

25

- **Keep your promises.** It may sound intuitive, but the key here is to only make the promises you can keep and reliably keep the promises you make. This speaks volumes to your integrity. Breaking promises is a major contributor to customer dissatisfaction and departure.

For example, you call your cable company for service repairs and they promise a technician will be at your residence the following day between 10:00 a.m. and noon. It is now mid-afternoon the next day and still no service technician has arrived. To add to the frustration, you do not even get a courtesy update call. The technician finally shows up at 4:00 p.m. and tells you his last job took longer than expected. How does that make you feel? Your trust in the cable company is likely diminished. Do you call the company and share your dissatisfaction with their service or do you cancel your service and find another provider—sharing your negative experience with friends and co-workers? Research suggests you will do the latter—which damages the company's reputation and much-desired loyalty from its customers.

- **Be respectful and respectable.** These are the precursors to being respected. Ensure that both in and out of the presence of your customers—internal and external—you speak and behave respectfully toward them. Paraphrasing the late Stephen Covey, do not go to Mary to confess the sins of Larry. Gossip does not contribute to resolving issues and certainly does not build positive relationships. It also damages your integrity, which is difficult to rebuild.

- **Maintain a "can-do" attitude.** Customers respond positively to service professionals who focus on how something can be done, as opposed to why it can't be done. Most often, reasons something cannot be done end up sounding like excuses to the customer.

I was traveling to a conference a few years back, and upon arriving late to the hotel, I was informed the room type I had reserved was not available. I shared that since I would be hosting a business meeting in the room, the additional space was particularly important. The front desk representative called over the manager and quickly apprised him

26

of the situation. When I shared again why I required that additional space, the manager replied, "Let me see how I can make that happen for you." What a positive, encouraging response. Ultimately, I did not get the exact room type I had originally reserved but did get sufficient accommodations for my needs. When we are satisfied with the outcome of a service breakdown, most of us put those experiences in our memory banks and share them with others. That is the kind of PR you want.

- **Make regular "pit stops."** Check in on your customers (internal and external) between normal interactions. Find out how your product or service is working for them, and explore how else you may be of assistance. This valuable customer feedback provides an opportunity to continue building those important relationships.

- **Value our differences.** Every individual has their own history of experiences and expectations regarding customer service. Therefore, it is important that customers not feel they are being forced into a one-size-fits-all situation. Value what each customer represents to your organization, and work to satisfy their unique needs to the extent possible.

In summary, positive customer relationships are at the heart of successful businesses. Customers leave organizations for understandable reasons. But there are effective strategies to create that essential customer loyalty, so that no one leaves you because of poor service, communication or attitude.

Remember—maintaining positive relationships with your customers is undoubtedly the greatest contributor to a strong competitive business advantage.

Chapter Review Questions

1. The primary reason customers leave businesses is that they:
   a. Got a better deal somewhere else
   b. Were treated with indifference by the owner, manager or an employee
   c. Moved away from the area
   d. Were dissatisfied with the product or service

2. Which of the following is not a reason to build strong customer relationships?
   a. To better support the customer
   b. To minimize the impact of service errors
   c. To be able to share with management the probable customer impact of proposed changes
   d. To ensure service breakdowns will never occur

3. The reason more than 50 percent of customers choose to leave a business is poor products or services.
   a. True
   b. False

4. David's mother told him she would leave work in time to watch his 4:30 p.m. ballgame but actually arrived at 5:00 p.m. Which statement best describes this situation from a customer service perspective?
   a. David knows his mother is always late.
   b. David's mother either worked late or was stuck in traffic.
   c. David's mother made a promise she did not keep.
   d. David's mother did her best to keep her promise.

5. "Sharing the Pain/Gain" refers to:
    a. Customers finding joy in your successes and empathizing with you when you fall short of an objective
    b. Letting your customers recognize that they can be the source of service breakdowns
    c. Updating your supervisor when customer activities are successful as well as when they are unsuccessful
    d. None of the above

6. "Synergy" is defined as: when two or more people working together create an increase in output value.
    a. True
    b. False

7. Which of the following is true?
    a. Customers usually do not tell the business when they are dissatisfied.
    b. Treating your customers with fairness and respect contributes very little to their overall loyalty.
    c. Customers are not likely to share their business complaints via social media.
    d. Business success is really not associated with customer referrals.

8. How can a positive customer relationship contribute to your personal recognition?
    a. It contributes significantly to your feelings of individual accomplishment.
    b. It guarantees you will get that next promotion.
    c. It lets your co-workers know who the most successful Customer Service Professional is.
    d. It will likely result in a special performance bonus for you.

9. Customers typically accept that they may receive differing information, depending on which of your company's Customer Service Professionals they interact with.
   a. True
   b. False

10. If a product or service is guaranteed, it indicates:
    a. The product won't break or service commitments will be fulfilled precisely as stated.
    b. This is just a marketing statement as it is impossible to satisfy everyone.
    c. The product or service is so dependable or of such excellent quality that the provider is willing to stand behind it.
    d. If the customer becomes dissatisfied after the purchase, they can expect to be caught in a "Your call is important to us" nightmare.

11. Customers never want to be bothered with extra communication, so to be safe, when a service breakdown occurs, you should not provide any updates until the breakdown is finally resolved.
    a. True
    b. False

12. The highest form of customer disrespect is:
    a. Dishonesty
    b. Setting prices too high
    c. Slow response times
    d. Delivery delays

13. Instead of ignoring our differences, we should find ways to value them.
    a. True
    b. False

14. Customer "pit stops" include:
    a. Checking in with your customers daily
    b. Sending customers their monthly invoice on time
    c. Exploring how your product or service is working for them
    d. Avoiding asking questions that you don't want answered

15. What can the Customer Service Professional do to avoid customers feeling they are being taken advantage of?
    a. Share your expertise in understandable terms.
    b. If unsure how to rectify a situation, confer with other subject matter experts in your company.
    c. Ensure your customers have all questions satisfactorily answered.
    d. Give your customers no reason to doubt your honesty by always being truthful.
    e. All of the above

CHAPTER 3

Insight into Customer Behaviors

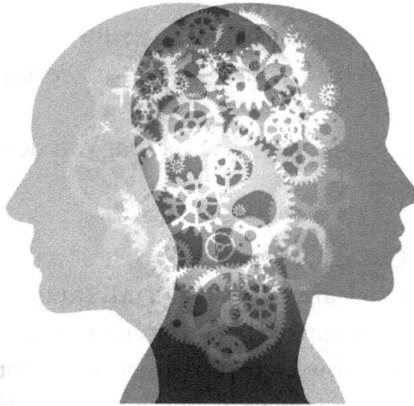

Behaviors are driven by our attitudes toward people, places and things. The stronger our attitude toward something or someone, the stronger and more consistent the behaviors toward that person or thing. In the example shared earlier, as a former smoker, I don't have to think about not lighting a cigarette. I have such a strong negative attitude toward smoking that the thought of doing so is repugnant.

On the other hand, I have worked hard to lose 20 pounds repeatedly and soon thereafter regained the weight. Why does that happen so frequently? I manipulated my behavior for the short term but did not change my attitude toward diet and nutrition.

> **Bottom line: You can change your attitudes with knowledge and the motivation to do so, which then changes your behavior.**

Our attitudes are rooted in four primary factors:

- Needs
- Personality
- Values
- Knowledge

While we may be "prewired" (born) with certain needs and personality traits, our experiences over time will impact our overall attitudes, both positively and negatively. Let's delve into each of these factors.

Needs

Every human being has needs. Some are **innate**—needs with which we are born. For example, we don't need to learn the need for food and warmth. This explains why a newborn baby quickly begins to suckle for nourishment or snuggles closely with its mother or father for warmth. Other needs are developed over time—these are known as **acquired** needs. While there are countless acquired needs, the ones that will contribute significantly to helping you understand your customers include:

- **Need for esteem.** People have a need to feel good about who they are and to be respected. Esteem is the human desire to be not only accepted but valued by others. Helping the customer feel good about themselves with every interaction is an excellent relationship-building opportunity.

Take for example a store that boldly advertises that 5 percent of all sales go to support U.S. military veterans. While this is certainly considered good "corporate citizenship," the customer feels good as well—increased esteem—knowing they are supporting a most worthwhile cause. Find ways to enhance people's self-esteem by discerning what their level of need is and accommodating it—to the extent possible—while not neglecting other customers' needs.

- **Need for affiliation.** Individuals with a need for affiliation enjoy social relationships and have a need to belong. People in this category respond positively to personal attention and supportive behavior. They tend to reach out to others with encouragement and are often eager to please. As a customer, this individual is often willing to work for and accept alternatives. The downside is that their proclivity to social interaction can detract from focusing on the issue at hand.

In one of our customer service training courses, a student shared that every month, a particular elderly customer would call her to discuss his bill. She said that the first couple of times, she was frustrated because he kept asking the same questions. But she soon realized it wasn't his bill that was important; it was the conversation they had. She learned he had no family, and this monthly call was a chance to connect with a familiar voice and someone who treated him with respect and care. Be aware of people's need for affiliation and accommodate it—to the extent you can—and still support other customers in the fashion they deserve.

- **Need for achievement.** The person with a high need for achievement likes to solve problems. They are motivated by winning and they like rewards—for what they represent, not necessarily the reward itself. These individuals may be both a blessing and a curse for the Customer Service Professional. On one hand, they are not deterred by a challenge, but on the other hand, may want to work toward a solution that is excessive for the current situation.

Imagine you call a customer because they did not accurately complete your company's online order form. All you require is a little additional information. On the phone, the customer goes into great detail regarding how you could modify the form and provides several process improvement recommendations. The customer likely wasn't as concerned with fixing the form and process for themselves, but felt a sense of achievement by sharing their depth of knowledge on the subject. These types of customers are a fountain of process improvement suggestions, but you have to temper their contribution if it eats up more time than you can afford. Refer them to your company's website where suggestions (hopefully) can be offered. The key is to actually review and consider that input and acknowledge the customer for their thoughts and time.

- **Need for power.** People with a high need for power like to be in control and respond well when addressed formally. They tend to be punctual and prefer things well organized and clearly explained. When working with such people, the Customer Service Professional must particularly focus on being **correct** in their messaging, versus being **right.** This customer type will not respond well to a Customer Service Professional vying for who is "more right." A "you first, then me" approach is much more effective.

Recently, I was flying home from a client engagement and waited an extraordinarily long time in the airline check-in line while another passenger spoke with the agent. He was very loud and demanding. He insisted that the "lady he spoke to on the phone" guaranteed he was booked on this flight, yet his reservation was not in the airline's system. He was verbose and taking a lot of time. The airline employee remained polite, used a soft voice, and addressed him as "Mr." in their conversation. Ultimately, she found a seat for him and apologized for any inconvenience while she resolved the issue. She went the extra mile to not prove that the customer, in this case, may have been wrong.

In another situation, I was waiting in a lengthy line for security screening at a major airport. A fairly young TSA agent walked up and down our line shouting, "Tighten up my line!" Obviously, it wasn't "his" line, though he was in charge of moving the line along. He could have been equally effective using a more pleasant voice and demeanor. He appeared to enjoy his position and authority a little too much, satisfying his need for power.

Most people develop some level of all of the acquired needs above, and, depending on the situation, one or more may appear dominantly—

and drive behavior accordingly. For the Customer Service Professional, this is important to understand so you can watch for signs of the needs at play and adjust your service strategies appropriately.

It is the desire to satisfy needs that **motivates** people to act. Basic motivation theory indicates that a person will exert themselves to achieve an objective if it satisfies a need. For example, if someone is hungry, they will make the effort to find food so it can satisfy their hunger. Customers exert effort to get what they feel they need, and the strength of that perceived need determines their commitment to satisfying it. Acknowledging this reality allows us to better understand, and thus satisfy, the needs of the customer.

As shared earlier, it is important to recognize that when a customer indicates what they "need," it may well be a "want." In other words, what the customer thinks they need is really what they want. These could be two entirely different things, and one may be more realistic to fulfill than the other. Your role—much like a doctor—is to **diagnose** the situation and **prescribe** what the customer actually needs. While this can be challenging, it does become easier with expanded customer service experience.

While working to satisfy customer needs, it is equally important to ensure you satisfy the needs of the business as well. Thus, the outcome of customer interactions should result in a **win** for the customer and a **win** for the company. If achieving a complete win-win outcome is impossible, the Customer Service Professional must collaborate with the customer to get as close as possible to this desired outcome. This approach provides for enhanced customer loyalty and long-term success for the organization.

Personality

Each of us has a personality that we develop over time. Simply defined,

> **Personality is a combination of psychological traits that describe a person and influence behavior.**

36

Many business professionals have completed some form of personality assessment during their careers. Among several instruments for assessing personality on the market, one that is widely used is the Myers-Briggs Type Indicator (MBTI), which breaks down personality into four pairs of personal preferences:

- **Extraversion vs. Introversion**—describes our preference for social interaction
- **Sensing vs. Intuition**—describes how we prefer to gather data
- **Thinking vs. Feeling**—describes our approach to decision-making
- **Judging vs. Perceiving**—describes our approach to people and tasks

Let's explore each of these preferences in more detail:

- **Extraversion vs. Introversion**

Extraversion. Extraverts tend to be energized by being around people. They enjoy engaging with people and often experience loneliness when not in contact with others. Customers who are extraverted can be more talkative and may want to continue communicating beyond the time necessary to address an issue. Often referred to as "ready-fire-aim," Extraverts may jump to a conclusion before they have all the necessary information. When working with a person who appears to be extraverted, a good approach is to assure key facts, details and options were not missed and conclude the conversation with a summary of next steps, responsible parties and timing.

Introversion. Introverts often find their energy sapped when around people. They typically seek quiet time in order to recharge their batteries. Customers who are more introverted are excellent listeners. They think through issues quite well but can be hesitant to move toward closure. It is typical for an Introvert to backtrack and review earlier points in a conversation. It is the Customer Service Professional's responsibility to ensure sufficient detail is provided to allow closure for this customer.

- **Sensing vs. Intuition**

  Sensing. The Sensor relies on experience and information for decision-making. This individual is practical and pays attention to details. Since a Sensor tends to make few factual errors, the Customer Service Professional must ensure they have accurate information readily available. The Customer Service Professional may find it more tedious to work with this customer because of the level of detail expected. On the other hand, engaging with this type of customer will encourage the Customer Service Professional to maintain high skill levels and preparedness.

  Intuition. While the Sensor may be considered an inside-the-box thinker, the Intuitive is more likely to say, "What box?" They rely on possibilities and inspiration, focus on the big picture, and readily work with complex issues. An Intuitive will often recommend viable solutions to an issue, which can be a challenge for the Customer Service Professional, as those solutions may not be available or may be too costly to implement. Once again, the Customer Service Professional must find the balance that meets both the customer's and the organization's needs.

- **Thinking vs. Feeling**

  Thinking. The Thinker tends to base decisions on logic. This individual is typically straightforward, brief and businesslike. There can appear to be little room for niceties, as they may tend to act impersonally and may seem a little cold or standoffish. The Thinker is a good analyst who makes a great ally to the Customer Service Professional, though building a warm relationship can be challenging.

  Feeling. The Feeler often bases decisions on values and the perceived needs of others. They are supportive in their interactions and tend to be naturally friendly. They work to ensure that the needs of all concerned are satisfied to the extent possible. For the Customer Service Professional, building an ongoing relationship is easier with a Feeler. However, this customer may also present a challenge, since they may detract from solving problems, favoring instead to maintain harmony, which doesn't necessarily get their needs met.

- **Judging vs. Perceiving**
  Judging. The Judger is typically planful—decisive and self-regimented. They make decisions easily, while focusing on closure—completing the task. They are well organized and contribute to finding solutions quickly, which is a great asset to the Customer Service Professional. Because of this customer's planning and organizational skills, the Customer Service Professional must be detail-oriented in their interactions with a Judger.
  Perceiving. The Perceiver is typically tolerant and spontaneous. They may struggle with details and tend to seek more data, delaying decisions longer than the Customer Service Professional would like. This customer often puts things off until the last minute, which makes closure on issues difficult. The Customer Service Professional must do more handholding to ensure the customer has what they need, recognizing the Perceiver may feel uneasy even after a decision is made.

It is important to remember that there are **no bad personalities,** and that personalities point out tendencies in groups of people—not absolutes for anyone. Lastly, individuals control their personalities, and not vice versa. And don't forget—you have a personality too!

Values

During the formative years of our youth, we develop a sense of what is right, what is wrong and what is important to us, thus creating our personal values. We do this based on our interactions with those around us. Family, friends and even strangers can influence our personal value systems. Concisely defined,

Values are the central truths, laws or beliefs from which arise the social rules of conduct. This includes our conduct as well as the conduct of others.

Our values determine how we treat one another and, equally importantly, how we treat ourselves. The strength of these values determines our adherence to them and the stress we experience when we violate them. A list of one's personal values can be lengthy. When our organization, the National Customer Service Association, works with clients to develop a departmental or organizational "shared values" list, it is not unusual for a focus group to brainstorm 30–40 value terms. We then work with them to narrow this list to several overarching values that the group supports.

From the Customer Service Professional's perspective, the following three foundational values are extremely powerful in effective bidirectional customer interactions:

- **Respect.** When you truly respect someone, you treat them in a manner that makes them feel good about themselves—in a positive, supportive way—both in and out of their presence. You think in terms of being respectful and respectable—respectful in your actions toward others, and respectable in how your behaviors cause others to treat you. It is often said that when we disrespect another, we have first disrespected ourselves—in other words, violated our personal values. Customers who truly feel respected will return that respect to you.

- **Honesty.** Honesty is treating others with fairness and truthfulness. Customers expect—and actually should demand—honesty from any business. Once they feel a sense of untruthfulness (a lie, manipulation, not sharing needed information up front, etc.), the likelihood of that customer returning to your business becomes very remote. People are better equipped to deal with the truth—regardless of its content—than some fiction concocted to make them feel better. A word of caution about being "brutally honest." Unfortunately, the emphasis can shift to brutal and the honest part isn't received—lost in the emotion of brutality. Avoiding brutal conversations is an exceptionally good idea—a respectful conversation is always a must.

- **Trust/Integrity.** Trust and integrity go hand in hand. People trust someone who displays integrity. The root of these two values is simply doing what you committed to do. A reminder of an excellent definition for the Customer Service Professional is:

> **Integrity is doing what you say you will do, even when no one is watching, regardless of the cost.**

Again, make the promises you can keep and keep the promises you make. Many of us have been victims of a promise that was not fulfilled. We were promised a product or service on a specific date, and it was not delivered. At that point, any reason sounds like an empty excuse. And when it comes from a Customer Service Professional, it can severely damage customer loyalty. In actuality, there may be valid reasons a commitment cannot be fulfilled. It is incumbent upon the Customer Service Professional to know this at the earliest opportunity and to communicate the status as soon as possible to the customer. Remember, people often give trust as a gift . . . the first time. Once trust is violated, substantial time and effort is required to earn it back—**if** the customer is willing.

It is important to remember that values are not a sometimes, "when it's convenient" kind of thing. These principles govern behavior 24/7. The good news is that you can work to strengthen your values and their positive influence on your behavior.

Knowledge

The last foundational factor influencing our attitudes that we will explore is knowledge. Here is a simple working definition:

Knowledge is what is learned in the process of doing and experiencing things.

We each have a unique set of experiences, and thus the expanse of our knowledge differs significantly. Knowledge gained from these experiences shape our attitudes. An interesting way to look at our experiences is by exploring various generational considerations.

WHAT YOU ARE IS WHERE YOU WERE WHEN

The drivers of human behavior we just explored impact every person—regardless of age. The nature of our needs, personality and values is greatly influenced by our individual experiences. Viewing these experiential influences in terms of generational "membership" can be helpful, assuming that individuals from the same generation were likely exposed to similar influences. While generational studies vary, most acknowledge the existence of five generations.

Generation	Born
Traditionals/Matures	1930–1945
Baby Boomers	1946–1963
Generation X	1964–1981
Millennials	1982–1995
Generation Z	1996–Present

Research suggests that our values, needs and even personalities are shaped largely by the experiences of our formative years—typically through age 12. Some current studies indicate they can extend up to age 25, though for our purposes, we will consider formative years to end approximately with age 12.

An article written many years ago by Morris Massey entitled "What You Are Is Where You Were When" argues just this—that what we were

42

exposed to during our formative years largely determines who we are today. Examples of key influencers include:

- Formative events: wars, the Space Race, technological advances, 9/11
- Heroes: sports figures, musicians, presidents, parents
- Television shows: Lawrence Welk, Andy Griffith, "The Simpsons," reality TV, competition shows
- Spending styles: save and pay, buy now and pay later, purchase online
- Technology: single-line dial phone, cell phone, texting, social media, virtual interactions

What does this mean for the Customer Service Professional? Here are some considerations for each generational group:

Traditionals/Matures. Relationships are especially important, and integrity is an absolute. They show an elevated level of brand loyalty and thus expect that the "brand" will be loyal to them. Their preference is "brick and mortar" and not "click and order"—they like to see and feel what they are purchasing. Desire to use technology is limited. Payment is typically "in full" and they are not particularly impressed with credit card deals. They focus more on needs than wants.

Tips for dealing with traditionals/matures:
- Recognize they have a propensity toward "technophobia" (fear of technology). So, the Customer Service Professional must provide ample information and necessary instruction and allow for a possible adjustment period.
- Be flexible with additional time it may take them to accept change.
- Show respect for their experience to help foster a strong working relationship.
- Consider them valued partners, and they will be eager to share their knowledge and experience. We can learn a great deal from traditionals/matures.

43

Baby Boomers. This group likes **traditional media** and is more comfortable with technology. Often, appearances are important. They may have a "he who dies with the most toys wins" mentality. Baby boomers tend to like quick fixes to problems—the easier the better. They are comfortable paying on credit and often find "0% financing" offers appealing. This group can be more inclined to satisfy their wants versus their needs.

Tips for dealing with baby boomers:
- Offer recognition and rewards for their patronage.
- Take your time—be friendly and get to know them.
- Recognize their tendency to play phone tag—initiate face-to-face interactions when possible.
- Boomers do not require formal signs of respect, but they do want to know their experience is respected.

Generation X. Generation X'ers tend to be **more self-confident.** You will find them wanting to negotiate. There is more focus on "green" products and making the world a better place. X'ers don't just expect honesty—they demand it. This group freely employs and enjoys technology. They are much more deliberate in their spending.

Tips for dealing with Generation X'ers:
- Get to the point in conversations. Avoid hyperbole and cliché, as they can be irritants.
- Understand they expect you to use technology to communicate effectively.
- Recognize that it may take time to earn the respect and trust of a Generation X customer—they are seldom given as a gift.
- Provide only the details requested, as they typically feel quite capable of working through issues.

Millennials. This generation **lives technology.** They are extremely optimistic, and often believe they can do anything. Spending their parents' money is acceptable, and they often influence their parents' buying trends. Millennials typically work to live—don't live to work. They are into experiences and authenticity. They know "real" when they see it. It is important to talk with millennials, not to them.

Tips for working with millennials:
- Show knowledge and empowerment to provide what is needed. Millennials are reassured by the presence of an authority figure.
- Be prepared for lofty expectations when working through issues. They want authenticity in people and products and feel comfortable challenging others.
- Partner with them when addressing problems.

Generation Z. This generation has been shaped by a post-9/11 world and our war on terror. They tend to be conservative with their money. The oldest Z's are working and saving what they earn. They do not like debt. When faced with a problem, **they take action.** These individuals are the "now" (Google) generation and expect information immediately through their handheld devices. Slow and cumbersome processes can be irritants. For the Customer Service Professional, this means using the media (and speed) they use and trust.

Tips for working with Generation Z:
- Be prepared for many questions and challenges in working through issues.
- Recognize that Generation Z'ers may not be equipped with complete or accurate information. As my doctor says, he has a challenging time competing with "Dr. Google."
- Remember, as discussed earlier, the customer is not always right, so proceed thoughtfully.
- Discover ways to make your interactions and processes as efficient and timely as possible.

In this chapter we addressed the primary elements that influence behavior. Obviously, customers and their needs are **not one-size-fits-all.** For the Customer Service Professional to more effectively serve, understanding the drivers behind their customers' (and their own) behavior is critical.

Chapter Review Questions

1. Sarah is very friendly during her customer interactions; however, in their absence she speaks negatively of them. What is likely occurring?
   a. Sarah is manipulating her behaviors in the presence of customers.
   b. Sarah does not possess an attitude of service.
   c. Sarah may have a high need for power.
   d. All of the above

2. Innate needs are learned.
   a. True
   b. False

3. Which of the following is not considered an acquired need?
   a. Need for affiliation
   b. Need for esteem
   c. Need for achievement
   d. Need for sustenance

4. Tim volunteers at the local animal shelter because it makes him feel good to help. Which of the following needs describes the source of his behavior?
   a. Need for social engagement
   b. Need for esteem
   c. Need for achievement
   d. Need for recognition

5. Which personality trait might best fit a customer who is very loud and boisterous?
   a. Feeler
   b. Extravert
   c. Perceiver
   d. Introvert

6. When considering personalities, Thinkers tend to be influenced by logic, while Feelers tend to be influenced by emotion.
   a. True
   b. False

7. When a service breakdown occurs, which customer personality preference is more apt to lead to outside-the-box solutions?
   a. Extraversion
   b. Intuition
   c. Perceiving
   d. Judging

8. Which of the following is not a key factor that influences our attitudes?
   a. Personality
   b. Initiative
   c. Needs
   d. Values

9. Most people develop some level of many acquired needs.
   a. True
   b. False

10. Which of the following describes the objective of basic human motivation?
   a. Satisfying a need
   b. Being honest
   c. Serving others
   d. Innate personality

11. If we're being really honest, some individuals just have bad personalities.
   a. True
   b. False

12. When you treat customers based primarily upon your emotions, which personality trait are you exhibiting?
   a. Perceiving
   b. Sensing
   c. Introversion
   d. Feeling

13. Chris sharing negative comments to Mary about a co-worker, Steve, is a violation of respectfulness.
   a. True
   b. False

14. What is a good meaning of integrity?
   a. Being judgmental
   b. Doing what you say you will do
   c. Avoiding conflict
   d. Going the extra mile

15. According to Morris Massey, which of these influenced us during our formative years?
    a. Significant events such as wars
    b. Who we identified as heroes
    c. What we watched on television
    d. Available technology
    e. All of the above

16. Which of the following is most accurate regarding personal values?
    a. Principled behavior is grounded in strong values.
    b. Customers are not likely to be concerned about a company's values.
    c. It is important to do what is right only f someone might observe you.
    d. Whether or not we should adhere to our values depends on the situation.

17. The fact that people—employees and customers—have vastly different experiential circumstances is cause to "customize" your approach to individuals.
    a. True
    b. False

18. Generational studies suggest people can be placed into what five categories?
    a. Traditionals/Matures, Post-War Boomers, Generation W, Millennials and Generation Z
    b. Veterans, Baby Boomers, Generation X, Millennials and Generation Y
    c. Traditionals/Matures, Baby Boomers, Generation X Millennials and Generation Z
    d. Matures, Boomers, Generation X, Realists and Generation Y

19. It is critical for the Customer Service Professional to interact with each generation in the same manner.
    a. True
    b. False

20. Which of the following is the most accurate?
    a. Millennials have a "take-it-or-leave-it" attitude toward technology.
    b. Realists tend to have a better understanding of life events in general.
    c. Generation X'ers enjoy hyperbole and cliché.
    d. Matures believe that integrity is an absolute.

21. Bottom line, you can change your attitudes given the knowledge and motivation to do so.
    a. True
    b. False

CHAPTER 4

Engaging in Successful Communication

The ability to communicate professionally and effectively is absolutely essential to customer satisfaction and loyalty. In this chapter we will explore communication and steps you can take to enhance your ability to be the best communicator possible.

Interpersonal Communication Process

What are the mechanics of communication? Diagram 4-1 illustrates the process we follow in communicating with one another.

- **Sender.** Someone initiates the communication. The sender is the person who begins the process, and they determine who will be the intended receiver(s) of the communication.
- **Encode.** The sender transforms their thoughts into a message, conveying what they intend to communicate. The format could be oral, written or expressive, such as a picture.
- **Medium.** The sender chooses what modality to utilize to transmit the message to the receiver(s). If the message is in oral form, the medium could be face-to-face, or electronic technology such as a phone call, voicemail or virtual meeting. If the message is in written form, it could be delivered in hardcopy or electronically, such as a text message or email.
- **Receiver.** This is the intended recipient of the sender's message. There may be multiple receivers, depending on the nature of the message.

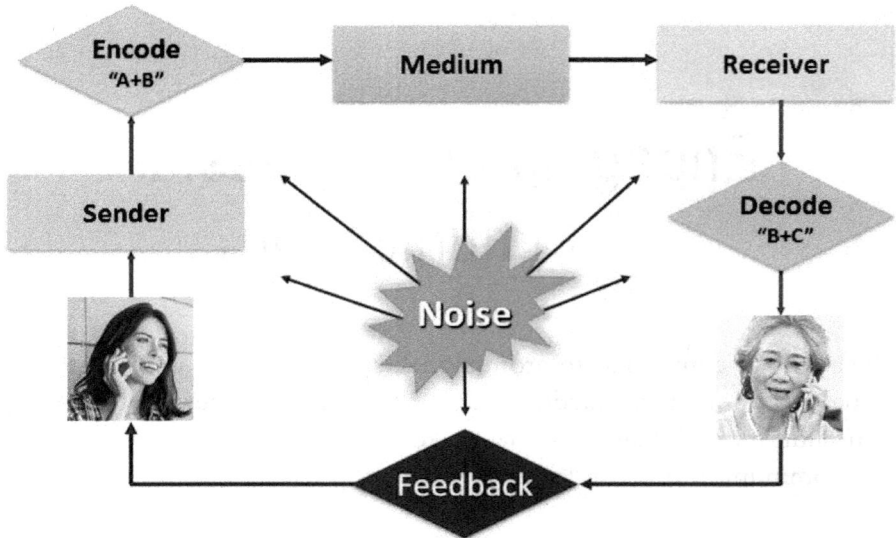

DIAGRAM 4-1

- **Decode.** Once the receiver has obtained the message, they must now decode or interpret it. In the diagram, the sender intended to transmit the message "A+B"; however, the receiver interpreted the message as "B+C." Unfortunately, our communications are too often misinterpreted in this stage. This is primarily associated with written communication.
- **Feedback.** Effective communication provides a means for the recipient to seek any desired clarity on the message. The more generic the message and the larger the audience, the more vague the message becomes, with few feedback options for clarification. The feedback link is essential to ensure expectations are understood and managed accordingly.
- **Noise.** This is the reason that intended messages are not identical to received messages. We will elaborate on "noise" in the following pages.

Why Communication Breaks Down

As we just discussed, recipients do not always get the intended message. This is due to several factors:

- **Too many links in the chain.** If you have ever played the game where you whisper a message into someone's ear and they whisper it to the next person and so forth, until the last person announces the message they heard, you know the last version is never the same as the original message, and often, is hilariously inaccurate. This is because each person receives only part of the message, filling in the rest with their imagination. In the business world, as communiqués are passed down in different forms, the original message can become greatly muddled, if not lost entirely.

- **Undefined expectations.** In this case, the recipient lacks complete information to deliver what the requestor expected. For example, you are facilitating a workshop on customer service. You take your PowerPoint file on a flash drive to the copy shop. You tell the print department employee you need 30 copies of the handouts, collated and stapled. When you return to pick up your copies, you discover each slide was printed on a separate page, single-sided and stapled at the top middle. What you actually wanted was two slides per page, double-sided and stapled in the upper left corner. Did you get your handouts? Yes, but not the handouts you wanted. Anytime we receive a request, it serves us well to ensure that the specifics are understood. When we are the requestor, it is important to consider what the recipient needs to know in order to complete the task as expected. Not fully understanding what the customer wants will likely result in a dissatisfied customer.

- **Failure to consider differences in communication skills.** We all have varying skills in numerous disciplines. Communication is no different. This is especially true when it comes to modern technology. Reflecting back on the generational differences we discussed earlier, we shouldn't be surprised to learn that many traditionals/matures may be challenged in using current electronic devices and applications. And

53

younger people—though skillful with modern technology—may lack a strong understanding of business writing. For the Customer Service Professional, it is imperative that communication strategies fit your intended audience.

- **Noise.** As Diagram 4-1 illustrates, "noise" is a pervasive phenomenon that often disrupts effective communication. Let's explore "noise" in more detail.

NOISE: BARRIERS TO EFFECTIVE COMMUNICATION

When we think of "noise," actual sound immediately comes to mind. This is not the only example, though, so let's explore the various forms of "noise" and their impact on effective communication.

- **Sound.** The typical "noise" we tend to think of. Most of us have fallen victim to the sounds of a crowded restaurant, heavy traffic, etc. In these situations, hearing and being heard can be a struggle. Listening is strained, as background sounds interfere with receiving the correct message. These interferences require that we adjust our communication approach—method and location—to ensure the intended message is received.

- **Filtering.** When employees are reluctant to share unpleasant news with their supervisor, they might filter the message by modifying it to more favorable terms (maybe even leaving out the "bad" news), so it is, hopefully, better accepted. This happens most often when there is a poor supervisor-subordinate relationship. When it comes to the customer, truthfulness is an absolute. If a customer suspects, or worse, discovers, the Customer Service Professional has not been fully honest, that relationship is likely doomed. When the relationship is positive, however, the customer is apt to tolerate occasional setbacks (not including dishonesty, however) and work with the Customer Service Professional to find resolutions.

- **Selective Reception.** In this case, the recipient hears what they want to hear, not the entire message communicated. Consider customer surveys as an example. We commonly focus only on the negative—hopefully constructive—comments shared. While such feedback can represent opportunities to improve the business, it should be balanced with the positive comments as well. You can learn and grow from both. For the Customer Service Professional, care must be taken, for example, to not let a lone negative comment from a customer influence future interaction with that customer. Instead, learn and grow from what is shared.

- **Emotion.** When individuals are emotional, they do not hear all that is being said. The more emotional the person, the more challenging it becomes to work through an issue. We will discuss this topic further when we explore **effective listening strategies.**

- **Information Overload.** Today, information comes at us quickly, from multiple sources, nonstop. Walk into any business meeting and you will likely see the "participants" on their phones, emailing or texting others outside the meeting. When questioned why they are engaged in these activities during the meeting, they often explain that "multitasking" is integral to their job. In reality, no one is wired to multitask. Our brains allow us to perform one high-level cognitive task at a time. So, when we are in a meeting and start looking at our phone, we are no longer engaged in that meeting. Neither of those interactions gets 100 percent of our attention.

Sadly, many of us suffer from **"CPA"—continuous partial attention**—which occurs when we try to engage in multiple high-level cognitive tasks simultaneously. A serious and deadly example of CPA is texting and driving. We are seeing increased automobile accidents as a result of driver distraction due to unacceptable (and dangerous) use of cell phones. Most people do not realize that when they are driving down the interstate at 70 miles per hour, they are covering a distance of 103 feet per second! While looking at their phone for just three seconds, they have traveled more than 300 feet and have no real idea of what happened on the road during that time.

From a customer service perspective, it is critical to be 100 percent engaged with the customer. Otherwise, they feel unworthy of your time and will "vote with their feet." The key is to learn to **manage multiple priorities** and avoid fruitless attempts at multitasking.

- **Defensiveness.** When confronted with a problem, we sometimes fixate on proving we are **right** rather than seeking an **effective resolution.** When we do this, we ignore or reject opportunities to fix the situation. As a Customer Service Professional, your job is to facilitate a balanced solution—not lay blame. Again, being appropriate is much more important than being right.

- **Language/Jargon.** In this case, we are not talking about a foreign language. We are referring to the use of **company-specific terms.** Every business has its own short forms, abbreviations or acronyms for internal communication efficiency. But your customers need to fully understand what you are communicating in common terms and language. Using jargon may be viewed as intentionally confusing or intimidating to the customer and is a sure way to lose business.

- **Culture.** Individuals from other countries, regions of the United States, different religious beliefs, ethnicities and generations have their cultural differences. The role of the Customer Service Professional is to **recognize and appreciate these differences** and adjust communication accordingly. Customer service is not a one-size-fits-all proposition. Knowing and responding to your customers' cultural expectations is key to retaining them. If the Customer Service Professional regularly deals with customers of different cultures, specialized training to better communicate with them may be warranted.

Communication Styles

Because we are diverse, we employ different communication styles or approaches, including passive, aggressive, assertive and the all-too-familiar passive-aggressive approach.

- **Passive.** We allow things to happen or accept what other people do.

- **Aggressive.** We are ready and willing to fight, argue or use other forceful methods to succeed.
- **Assertive.** We are self-confident, decisive, firm and emphatic.
- **Passive-Aggressive.** We appear to accept what others do and later become willing to fight, argue or use other forceful methods.

While communication style may be reflected in all mediums of communication, typically style is more apparent during in-person communication. In other forms of communication, style may be subtler and more difficult to interpret.

The style we use typically depends on the situation—who we are communicating with, how much power we sense we have, and the importance of the outcome to us. The more powerful we feel and the more important the issue, the greater the likelihood that we become more aggressive in our communication. The less our perceived power and the importance of the issue, the more likely we are to take a more passive communication approach.

Ideally, all individuals should **adopt an assertive approach** to interpersonal communication, as it is the style most likely to lead to positive outcomes for all concerned. You should avoid a passive-aggressive approach always, because your customers can feel manipulated at worst, or just unsure of how you will respond. Feeling unsure about the Customer Service Professional's response leads to questions of integrity—and your relationship is likely doomed!

Here is a more complete, functional definition of assertiveness:

Assertiveness is the ability to communicate clearly, succinctly and persuasively what you want or need from another person or persons in a manner that produces a two-way, respectful conversation.

Assertive in-person communication, and to some extent virtual communication, is evidenced by the characteristics below. As you review the list, reflect on how you approach interpersonal communication. Some of these characteristics will become clearer by the end of this chapter.

- **Verbal.** Wants and feelings are clearly articulated. Assertive language leaves no doubt regarding the speaker's expectations. Since assertive communication is always respectful, this approach is always clear but never "brutal."
- **Nonverbal.** Attentive, active listening is exhibited.
- **Voice.** Speech is well modulated—firm, but warm. The volume is not too loud or soft, and easy to listen to.
- **Eyes.** Eyes are open with good—not uncomfortable—eye contact. Glancing away occasionally is preferred—never staring for a prolonged period of time.
- **Stance.** Posture is balanced and relaxed. Personal space is acknowledged and respected.
- **Hands.** Relaxed movement is maintained. We all know people who talk with their hands. Assertive communication involves minimal hand motion and a neutral position. We will explore **nonverbal communication** in greater depth below.

Each of us should strive to adopt this assertive communication style. When we are aggressive, we do not truly hear the other person and come off as dominating the conversation, which leads to lost customers. When we are passive, we are not truly heard by others and, therefore, provide little value. When we are passive-aggressive, we are not predictable and thus not trustworthy, and people will avoid us. For the Customer Service Professional, the only clear style for building and maintaining positive customer service relationships is an assertive one.

Communication Types or Mediums

In addition to styles, there are also several communication types or mediums—the method and manner in which you choose to communicate.

Your goal must be to maximize the effectiveness of your communication, regardless of the type of communication medium chosen.

We can define communication effectiveness as the extent to which the selected medium of communication allows both the sender and the receiver of the information to reach a **mutual understanding** of the intended message. Simply stated, was the message that the sender intended accurately received by the intended receiver?

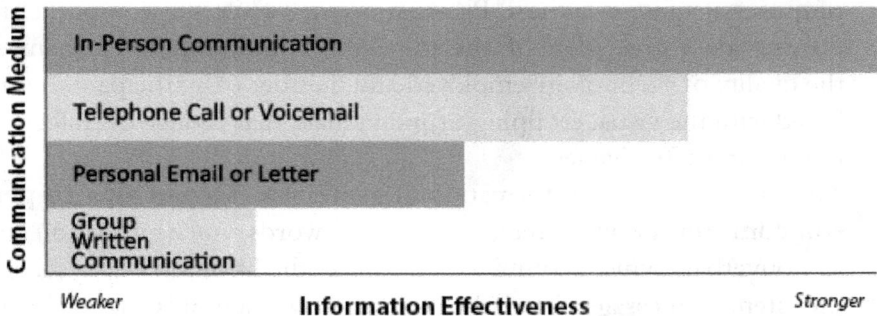

Communication Medium (vertical axis)

| In-Person Communication |
| Telephone Call or Voicemail |
| Personal Email or Letter |
| Group Written Communication |

Weaker — **Information Effectiveness** — Stronger

DIAGRAM 4-2

Diagram 4-2 depicts the level of effectiveness of various communications channels.

- A **written communication sent to a group** might take the form of a company bulletin or blast email. For example, to notify employees of an upcoming insurance enrollment period. Because this message is for numerous employees, it cannot contain personalized information. Additionally, because it only contains written words (or graphics), it lacks voice intonation and nonverbals.
- In the **personal email or letter,** information can be geared to a specific individual. Both are delivered to a specific recipient. Again, because you lack voice intonation and nonverbals, the effectiveness is on the weaker end. In both written types, you must count on the words being construed

literally. "Great" must mean exactly that and, for instance, not the disgusted sentiment which can't be interpreted in written communication.

- Even stronger information effectiveness is found in a **telephone call or voicemail.** In these situations, you have added voice intonation to the message, enhancing its effectiveness and subsequent understanding. Here, the intended meaning of "great" can be more clearly understood.
- When using **video communication,** you gain several additional cues not available in the above mediums. In today's business environment, using applications such as Zoom or Google Meet for communication purposes is quite common. Please note that while these applications do provide a great deal of the in-person communication dynamics, the quality of technology employed and number of participants, combined with the visual cropping of individuals, may reduce overall communication effectiveness.
- The highest level of information effectiveness emerges with **in-person communication.** Here, you have the words, voice intonation and all nonverbals, which, combined, maximize the likelihood of receiving the intended message. When dealing with customers, it is always best to use the strongest, most effective form of communication available— especially when complicated issues such as service breakdowns arise. The sterility of back-and-forth emails can cause additional confusion and thus impede the Customer Service Professional's service recovery efforts.

The work of Albert Mehrabian, a pioneer of communications since the 1960s and professor emeritus at UCLA, confirmed the significance of information effectiveness. Studying thousands of **in-person** conversations, Mehrabian discovered that the relative importance of conversational elements in causing the listener to fully understand a speaker's message are as follows:

- Words used: 7%
- Vocal tone: 38%
- Nonverbals: 55%

To ensure the message that was intended is the message received, you should strive to make communication in-person when possible. Second best is to employ virtual technology, followed by a telephone call. Writing—because of limited communication cues—should be your last choice, especially for sensitive and timely issues.

Nonverbal Communication

As we just discussed, nonverbal messages are an integral component of communication. Nonverbals reinforce and define the spoken word. They may even replace the spoken word. Nonverbals also provide feedback and assurance that we are listening. Simply defined,

> **Nonverbal communication is the movements, gestures and other physical signals that clarify or confuse the meaning of the verbal communication.**

Nonverbals can be confusing if they do not support the other parts of the communication. Take, for example, a boy asking his father if he can go down the street to play with a friend. The father replies "yes," while shaking his head "no." This was likely done in jest; however, it exemplifies that nonverbals can detract from the intended message. We might refer to nonverbals as either "contributors"—supporting the intended message—or "detractors"—inhibiting receipt of the intended message. Let's consider examples of each:

Detractors
- Crossed arms
- No or little eye contact
- Looking at watch
- Looking at phone
- Pointing finger

61

- Hands on hips
- Head shaking

When you exhibit one or more of these nonverbals, it detracts from the listener's ability to stay focused on the message. Instead, you find yourself wondering why the listener appears to not be listening or liking the message. This can derail your train of thought and the delivery of your intended message.

Other forms of nonverbals can enhance the interaction and contribute to an improved understanding of the intended message. Consider the following examples:

Contributors
- Relaxed posture
- Nodding with acknowledgement
- Good eye contact
- Intent focus
- Smiling
- Look of concern (as appropriate)

Note that "nodding with acknowledgment" is different than "nodding in agreement." When the listener is nodding their head, they are typically indicating they hear and understand what the speaker is saying. It is important that the speaker not misinterpret this as agreement with the message. Clarifying with the receiver whether the head nod means agreement or merely acknowledgement is appropriate.

As we just noted, **nonverbals are eight times more powerful** than the words we speak. The Customer Service Professional must understand that what the customer sees is far more important than what they hear. Ensuring your nonverbals match your spoken words is essential. Saying the word "yes" while nonverbally indicating "no" is unsettling to customers and may cause them to seek service elsewhere.

Voice Inflection

The intonation in your voice can also reinforce or modify the spoken word. How often do we hear the word "great" when the speaker means just the opposite? That is the power of voice inflection. In the written word, "great" has to be used literally—meaning good, wonderful, excellent, and nothing else. The reader only sees the word and does not hear the intended inflection that would cause it to mean terrible, dreadful or awful.

In phone calls and in-person interactions, intonation facilitates understanding of the message. It is important to recognize, though, that not all phones and devices transmit with equal clarity. Using your words literally is a safe bet on the phone. If something is awful—say it is awful.

Rate of Speech

All of us have listened to someone speak very slowly. Or at the other extreme, you're probably familiar with those disclaimers at the end of television and radio commercials that are so fast you cannot possibly pick up on the information.

The rate at which you speak is an important part of communication. Research suggests that the average person comprehends best at a rate of 140–150 words per minute. This allows us to hear all the words, pick up on any voice inflection and then effectively process the communication. Find a paragraph—or create one—that is 140–150 words in length. Time yourself reading the paragraph until you are able to complete it in approximately one minute. It is common to feel that this rate seems slow, but it is the optimal one for the listener. This is a good exercise, especially if you speak with customers on the phone. Speaking at 140–150 words per minute—especially when you feel compelled to move things along faster—will make you a much more effective and better-received communicator.

Listening

In face-to-face communication, how much time do you spend speaking versus listening? If we are honest with ourselves, most of us find we speak more than we listen. It is important to recognize that **we learn when we are listening,** not when we are speaking. Your customers can pick up on your lack of listening and will not feel valued by you and, by extension, your organization. Personal and professional growth demands we be effective listeners. It is also an integral part of assertive communication.

Here are some interesting statistics. The average person speaks at a rate of 125–150 words per minute. We comprehend up to 600 words per minute and we think at 1,000–3,000 words per minute. Because words are spoken to us much slower than we think, we often lose concentration and may not fully hear the speaker. Thus, it is critical that we engage in effective or **active listening.**

What constitutes effective listening?
- Maintaining good eye contact—however, not staring
- Paraphrasing—"speaking back"—as appropriate, to confirm what the speaker is saying and to show you are listening
- Using nonverbal affirmations—e.g., head nod, smile
- Avoiding distracting mannerisms—e.g., looking at your watch, phone, email
- Asking appropriate questions to seek clarity—not evaluate
- Balancing talking and listening—never interrupt
- Summarizing at the end of the other person's statement—to do's, next steps, responsible parties, timing

LISTEN MORE THAN YOU SPEAK

Research on face-to-face and telephonic communications in U.S. culture suggests that we spend most of our time either speaking or preparing to speak. As a result, people often do not feel fully heard. For a Customer Service Professional, a useful mantra might be, "Listen more than I speak." Listening positions you to learn from the customer and enables you to better serve them.

The highest form of listening is empathic listening, which involves listening beyond the words, intonation and nonverbals to recognize the speaker's emotion.

> **Empathic listening is listening and responding in such a manner as to virtually project yourself into the emotions of the other person.**

More simply stated,

> **Empathic listening is listening for feelings with your eyes.**

Recall that emotion is a type of "noise" and interferes with the successful transmission of the sender's intended message. Take, for example, an angry customer. As the Customer Service Professional, you might use your best efforts to provide a solution to satisfy what you perceive as the customer's needs. But the customer is not willing to accept it. Instead, they continue to speak loudly and emotionally. Why? Until you acknowledge the customer's condition—that they are upset—they will not be ready to accept any solution. You might say, "I can see you are upset, and I would be too in this situation." And it might take several moments of acknowledging their emotion to reach a point where you can provide an acceptable solution.

Remember, the customer is looking for recognition and validation of their current state. Once they are satisfied that you can relate to their emotion—whatever the cause—you will be able to proceed with assistance.

So, why is it important for the Customer Service Professional to engage in empathic listening? There are several advantages:
- Reduces tensions—offering solutions before the customer is ready to "hear" them only heightens the tension

- Provides for a release of emotions
- Allows for a sharing of the genuine issues
- Provides a safe zone—so the other person feels comfortable sharing the "why" of their feelings
- Builds trust and respect—you are seen as an understanding and caring partner

Sadly, some customers can become abusive in their choice of words or mannerisms. It is important that you understand your company's policy regarding how to respond if the dialogue becomes offensive. No Customer Service Professional should be expected to tolerate abusive behavior in any form.

As we have discussed, listening is far more than just **hearing.** Effective, active listening should be a routine for the Customer Service Professional. Make it an integral part of your attitude for service. Here is a summary of some highly effective listening habits:

- Listen attentively—use positive nonverbals.
- Do not interrupt unnecessarily—listen more than you speak.
- Respond versus react—it is more thoughtful, appreciated and productive.
- Clarify as necessary—use caution not to probe unnecessarily.
- Listen nonjudgmentally.
- Offer input as appropriate.
- Be empathic—recognize and acknowledge the emotion.

It takes a wide variety of skills to be an effective Customer Service Professional. At the top is the ability to **communicate effectively.** It permeates all we do and largely determines our success—or failure. Communication skills must, therefore, be learned and mastered by all Customer Service Professionals.

Chapter Review Questions

1. Feedback is not essential in the interpersonal communication process.
    a. True
    b. False

2. Which of the following is not a reason communication breaks down?
    a. Defined expectations
    b. Too many links in the chain
    c. Differences in communication skills
    d. Noise

3. Kendal only tells his customers what he thinks they want to hear. This is an example of what kind of communication "noise"?
    a. Actual sounds
    b. Filtering
    c. Emotion
    d. Information overload

4. Ideally, you should strive for which communication style?
    a. Passive
    b. Aggressive
    c. Passive-aggressive
    d. Assertive

5. The medium of communication you use has little impact on the overall effectiveness of your communication.
    a. True
    b. False

6. Brutal honesty is vital for successful in-person communication.
   a. True
   b. False

7. Charles must communicate with an upset customer. Which communication medium should Charles use that will provide the greatest level of "information effectiveness"?
   a. Written group communication
   b. Personal email or letter
   c. In-person meeting
   d. Telephone call or voicemail

8. Albert Mehrabian's research on interpersonal communication discovered which of the following had the most impact on in-person communication?
   a. Nonverbals
   b. Vocal tone
   c. Words used
   d. Attitude

9. Nonverbals only serve to clarify verbal communication.
   a. True
   b. False

10. Which of the following detracts from effective communication?
   a. Well-modulated voice
   b. Looking at watch
   c. Good eye contact
   d. Active listening

11. Which of the following can impact the effectiveness of virtual video communication?
    a. Skill of application user
    b. Number of participants
    c. Connectivity quality
    d. Unclear nonverbal cues
    e. All of the above
    f. None of the above

12. Nonverbal communication is defined as the movements, gestures and other physical signals that clarify or confuse the meaning of the verbal communication.
    a. True
    b. False

13. When speaking with a customer, which rate of speaking is best for being readily understood?
    a. 300–350 words per minute
    b. 200–250 words per minute
    c. 60–80 words per minute
    d. 140–150 words per minute

14. Which of the following may lead to ineffective listening?
    a. Balancing talking and listening
    b. Using positive nonverbals
    c. Remaining silent
    d. Paraphrasing as appropriate

15. You discover more about customers when you are:
    a. Speaking
    b. Listening

16. The simple definition of empathic listening is:
    a. Listening for feelings with your eyes
    b. Crying with someone
    c. Feeling sorry for the person
    d. Ignoring emotion to solve a problem

CHAPTER 5

Customer Interaction

In this chapter, we will delve into the specifics of direct-contact customer interactions. While not all customer contact is face-to-face, the following information can assist in serving all customers professionally and consistently. Several recommendations will incorporate concepts we have previously discussed, but are worthy of additional consideration.

Mindset

It is always important that the Customer Service Professional be positive in customer interactions. Starting a conversation with the word "no" is the first stage of failure in strengthening customer loyalty. Encouraging, optimistic interactions come from maintaining that can-do attitude of service. Treat your customers as though your job depends on them, because it does.

Being in control of yourself and the situation is extremely important. Think in terms of "locus of control." In other words, who controls your behaviors? If you, as the Customer Service Professional, let your emotions take control, there cannot be a positive outcome. This means never giving a customer permission to make you angry. Remember, they don't make you angry; becoming angry is your choice and will lead to disastrous consequences for customer satisfaction.

Always be prepared to go the extra mile. As former football player Roger Staubach says, "There are no traffic jams along the extra mile." Great opportunities await the Customer Service Professional who is willing to do more than just what is considered "sufficient." Always exceeding adequate—going that extra mile—is a surefire way to create and maintain loyal customers.

Appearance

You may have heard the saying "Dress for success." I prefer the saying "Dress for your customer." For businesses that provide or require a particular dress code, clothing is not really a concern. For others, there is another time-tested saying: "You don't get a second chance at first impressions." Think about businesses you visit. How did the customer service individual appear to you? Was their clothing appropriate for the business and setting—neat and clean? Poor grooming and dress can be a real turnoff for your customers. In today's work environment, Customer Service Professionals may have visible tattoos or body piercings. You should consider how your customers may view these—especially in light of the generational differences we discussed earlier.

When you feel good about your personal appearance, your customer interaction tends to be more positive. The bottom line: appearance can attract or deter customers.

Knowledge

As we've shared, knowing your job extremely well is vitally important. Not just enough to provide adequate service, but to put forth extra effort in serving your customers when possible. Learn enough to answer questions beyond your typical role. Learn what others do before and after you in your workflow. This will enable you to better handle a wider variety of customer inquiries.

What is your level of empowerment to handle customer concerns or complaints? Do you have to "check with the boss" before offering your customer what they want or a viable alternative? Customers prefer to work with a Customer Service Professional who can offer alternatives on the spot. Not doing so may cause your customers to question your knowledge and certainly your authority. It is also important to understand your organization's procedure for escalating customer issues when necessary.

Awareness

Especially important for in-person customer interactions is that the Customer Service Professional remain focused—watch for opportunities to serve. Recognize that some customers may be reticent to engage you, preferring instead to deal with things themselves.

GREETING

Look for nonverbals that indicate that the customer is confused or frustrated. Have you ever approached the service counter or checkout area of a business only to have one or more employees—who appear to be doing nothing—seem like they are ignoring you? When this occurs do you want to say, "Let me know if I am interrupting you"? You think to yourself, *These employees could use a reminder of the importance of customers.*

In face-to-face interactions, smile and acknowledge the customer when they are approximately 10 feet away, and greet them at 5 feet. Be warm and friendly, recognizing again that you are the company.

WORDS

Use the correct words in your interactions, such as:

- "Welcome to . . ."
- "My name is . . ."
- "How are you today?"
- "How may I be of service?"

Recall what we discussed regarding communication. Use a pleasant tone and measured rate of speech, and employ an assertive communica-

73

tion style. Watch for signs or sounds of anger or discontent—especially if the customer is using a raised voice.

SERVING

When speaking with your customer, providing accurate information is important. Ensure you actually know, versus think, you are correct. While thinking is always encouraged, unconfirmed information can result in unfulfilled expectations for your customer.

- Be extraordinary. Exceeding your customers' expectations is a sure path to gaining their much-sought-after loyalty.
- While you want to wow the customer, ensure you are not smothering them. Too much information, and little opportunity for them to respond, can contribute to their being dissatisfied with you and your organization.
- As we discussed earlier, it is critical that you make the promises you can keep and keep the promises you make. Offering a customer something that you know you may not be able to deliver is a clear path to disaster.
- Ensure that all facets of your customer interactions cause them to want to return. That is the ultimate reward for the Customer Service Professional.

CLOSING THE INTERACTION

- Use "building" statements:
  - "It's my pleasure."
  - "Thank you."
  - "Please come/call again."
  - "I/we appreciate your business."
- Confirm any next steps that may be necessary—for both you and the customer.
- The goal in the customer closing is to have them look forward to the next visit or contact.
- When needed, ensure you create a positive "handoff"—whether horizontal or vertical in the organization.

SPECIAL NEEDS

Pay special attention to any customers with special needs or ambulatory issues. While buildings typically comply with the Americans with Disabilities Act (ADA) requirements, access challenges may still exist. This can be especially difficult for individuals using wheelchairs, transport chairs, walkers or crutches. For example, while the entrance doors may be wide enough to accommodate assistive equipment, not all have automatic openers.

A couple of years ago, because of a temporary medical issue, I had to be pushed in a transport chair entering and exiting businesses. While my wife pushed, I would sometimes struggle to reach for the door. On more than one occasion, because of the small wheels, I almost fell forward out of the chair as she pushed me across a slightly elevated doorway threshold.

Here are some service considerations for interacting with a customer in a wheelchair or transport chair:
- Most importantly, treat them exactly as you would any other customer.
- Don't assume needs the customer does not express to you— avoid making any assumptions.
- Don't touch the wheelchair or transport chair unless the customer asks.
- Respect the customer's personal boundaries.
- Speak directly with the person—not at the person.
- Don't bend over or kneel to interact with the customer.
- Be watchful of anything that could make it challenging to navigate your facilities.

When the customer feels they are treated like every other customer, they will be satisfied and share their experience with others, which contributes to overall loyalty.

CUSTOMER BEHAVIOR MATRIX

As we discussed earlier, there are several factors that influence people's behavior. While insights into behavioral sources are important for the

Customer Service Professional, in direct-contact customer interactions you obviously don't have immediate knowledge of their personality type, needs, values or experiences.

There are, however, some straightforward customer cues you can tune into quickly in the conversation. For example, you can easily determine if the customer is outgoing or more reserved. And when offering recommendations, is the customer rigid—non-wavering in their expectations—or are they more flexible on viable solutions to their issue?

By combining these two behavioral spectrums, we can gain insight into four personality classifications, as shown in the Diagram 5-1 matrix.

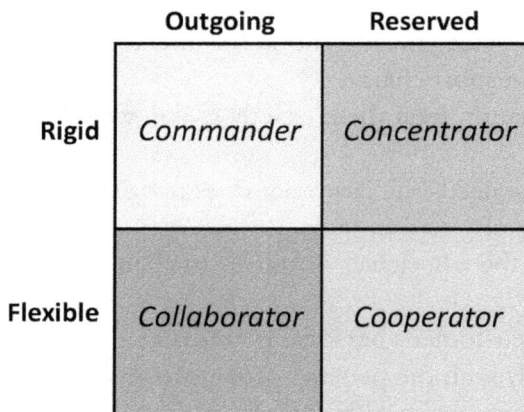

	Outgoing	**Reserved**
Rigid	*Commander*	*Concentrator*
Flexible	*Collaborator*	*Cooperator*

DIAGRAM 5-1

Commander. Commanders are **outgoing** and **rigid.**
- This customer commands attention and will not hesitate to use their power—real or perceived—to get what they want.
- They are courageous and unbending in their views.
- They can be vocal and loud and don't mind attracting attention.

Concentrator. Concentrators are **reserved** and **rigid.**
- Feeling shy and insecure, these individuals tend to keep a low profile and avoid drawing attention to themselves.

76

- They do know what they want and are meticulous in the pursuit.
- While normally cooperative, they will not hesitate to stand their ground when pressured or confronted.

Collaborator. Collaborators are **outgoing** and **flexible.**
- Because of their confidence and sophistication, these customers can easily become the center of attention.
- They do, however, accept reasonable ideas—collaborators can be persuaded.

Cooperator. Cooperators are **reserved** and **flexible.**
- This customer is known for their quiet demeanor and overall integrity.
- They are sincere, calm and have keen insight.
- They are able to see all sides of an issue and are willing to adjust their views, given adequate reason.

Yes, we can observe these behaviors early in a customer interaction, so how can the Customer Service Professional best work with each of these four types?

Dealing with Commanders
- Move to a secluded location if possible—away from the earshot of others who may be nearby.
- Let this customer talk themselves out—and listen fully to every comment.
- Be willing to compromise if you want to save the relationship. Sometimes that is a real big "if."
- You may find yourself having to over-apologize—even if you have done nothing wrong.
- Make sure to thoroughly document your interaction, as commanders may return to further discuss the issue or escalate it within your organization.

Dealing with Concentrators
- Acknowledge this customer for their understanding.
- Show appreciation for their suggestions.

77

- Work for a true win-win outcome—allowing you and the customer to succeed.
- Be prepared to deal with "why not" responses.
- Explain how your solution is beneficial to both parties.

Dealing with Collaborators

- Express confidence in finding a viable solution.
- Avoid confrontational communication—both verbal and nonverbal.
- Know your company's policies and apply them consistently.
- Do not underestimate the persistence of this customer.
- Always follow up with the collaborator to confirm the solution is satisfactory.

Dealing with Cooperators

- Be an active listener.
- Work to build a relationship—you want cooperators as customers.
- Acknowledge their understanding of the situation.
- Work in partnership for the highest level of a win-win outcome.
- Offer your sincere praise and gratitude for their overall cooperation.

Successfully Addressing Customer Issues

Confronting people leads to resistance.
Confronting problems leads to solutions.

As we discussed in Chapter 2, customers become dissatisfied for a number of reasons—not the least of which is how they are treated by you or someone in your organization. Some customers will leave and go elsewhere because of the product or service you are currently providing them. The Customer Service Professional's responsibility in each of these situations is to interact with the customer in a manner that shows your and your organization's commitment to customers. Let's review some techniques that will enhance your prospects of effective service recovery.

SERVICE RECOVERY TEMPLATE

The following elements, if used correctly, can work to repair a "broken" service issue and show your customers your genuine interest in satisfying their needs. You may choose to use some or all of the elements in the template, depending on the nature of the issue at hand.

- **Treat every customer with importance**
  a. They have influence over you and your organization—now and into the future.
  b. They provide valuable opportunities to improve your processes, products and services.
  c. With social media readily available, compliments, as well as complaints, seemingly travel at the speed of light. Work toward eliminating those complaints while increasing customer accolades.

- **Use words that people like to hear and have a beneficial calming effect**
  a. "Thank you for being so patient."
  b. "I agree this appears confusing."
  c. "Let me see how I can make that happen."
  d. "I will"; "I can"; "I would be happy to."
  e. "Yes, I understand."
  f. "It works better if we can . . ."
  g. "Yes, there are alternatives we can consider."
  h. "Is there anything else I can do?"
  i. And when the customer says, "Thank you," reply with something positive, like, "It's my pleasure." Refrain from replying with "No problem," as that can insinuate that customers feel they are some form of trouble for you.

    j.   Avoid using the word "No" at the beginning of a sentence at all times, as this signals to the customer that they are not likely to hear anything positive after that.

- **Actively listen**
  - a. Get the customer's name early in the conversation and address them in that manner during your conversation. This is the beginning of creating a relationship—people like to hear their names, and it personalizes the discussion.
  - b. Do not outtalk the customer—listen more than you speak.
  - c. Ask the customer to present the issue from their perspective.
  - d. Listen patiently—absolutely no arguing. Retain your locus of control, especially if the customer is or becomes emotional.
  - e. Remember that this is not personal—you may be dealing with the "final straw" of a sequence of issues the customer has experienced.

- **Ask questions**
  - a. Get details—again, from the customer's perspective.
  - b. Identify the problem—not a symptom of the problem.
  - c. Avoid getting caught up in exaggerated allegations by keeping your emotions under control.

- **Empathize—apologize**
  - a. Take responsibility for the situation—this will aid in moving toward a satisfactory conclusion.
  - b. Recognize and acknowledge the customer's frustration.
  - c. Share sincere regret that this matter has occurred.
  - d. View the issue from the customer's perspective—understanding how and why they may feel the way they do.

- **Clarify their request**
  - a. Ensure you know exactly what the customer wants—not just what you feel they need.
  - b. It can be helpful to "speak back" what the customer wants to ensure your understanding is accurate.

- **Offer alternatives**
  a. Identify options that may satisfy the customer.
  b. Resolution must be a win-win—satisfying what the customer needs while getting what your company needs.
  c. Work toward a compromise if you are unable to find a solution that satisfies all of the customer's and your organization's needs.

- **Thank the customer**
  a. Let them know you appreciate their working with you to resolve this issue.

- **Follow up**
  a. Contact the customer to verify the solution has worked for them. If it hasn't, explore what can be done to improve the situation.

- **When appropriate, pause or terminate proceedings**
  a. If emotions escalate during the proceedings, it may be necessary to take a break and resume after a reasonable time period.
  b. In no case should the Customer Service Professional tolerate or be expected to tolerate shouting, cursing or threats of any kind from a customer.
  c. If you determine the proceedings cannot continue—for any reason—inform the customer you are terminating the interaction and why.
  d. Immediately document in detail what occurred during the interaction.
  e. Share details of the proceedings with a supervisor or other manager—the procedure for doing so may be addressed in a company policy.
  f. When the customer is still unsatisfied, it may be necessary to escalate the situation.

- **Escalating customer concerns**
  a. Escalation occurs when the employee is not able—by issue or policy—to satisfy a customer's needs.
  b. Policies on the process for escalating customer issues vary by company, thus it is important that customer service personnel fully understand their company's customer escalation procedure.
  c. It is typical for the following conditions to warrant issue escalation.
     i. Customer threatening behavior of a personal nature
     ii. Serious threat of legal action against the organization
     iii. Request that is quite unusual or exceeds the employee's authority
     iv. Customer demanding to speak with a supervisor

Again, this is a very detailed service recovery template and can apply to customer service issues of all types and sizes. It is the Customer Service Professional's responsibility to select and apply the appropriate elements of this template to best fit a given situation.

Something else to consider: As a longtime member of Rotary International, an international service organization, we are provided with a copy of the "Four-Way Test." The Four-Way Test is a nonpartisan and nonsectarian ethical guide for Rotarians to use for their personal and professional relationships. Its four straightforward questions can serve the Customer Service Professional in building customer relationships that contribute to their long-term loyalty. The "test" follows:

In all we say and do:
1. Is it the truth?
2. Is it fair to all concerned?
3. Will it build goodwill and better friendships?
4. Will it be beneficial to all concerned?

As a Customer Service Professional, if you can answer "yes" to these four questions in each of your customer interactions, you should experience very satisfied and loyal customers.

Remember—customers are:
- The reason you are in business
- Never an interruption
- Drive improvement and innovation in your business
- Influence your organization's strategic direction
- Make tomorrow possible

In this chapter, we discussed many dimensions of customer interactions. Your organization may have procedural policies that contribute to positive customer interactions as well—which should be followed. As with all customer interactions, the overarching goal is to create customers for a lifetime.

Chapter Review Questions

1. When interacting with customers, which of the following is not part of a positive mindset?
    a. Maintaining a "can do" attitude
    b. Believing there are, indeed, traffic jams along the extra mile
    c. Recognizing your job exists because of customers
    d. Going beyond "sufficient" in your job responsibilities

2. Individual appearance can attract or deter customers.
    a. True
    b. False

3. Which of the following is true regarding your personal appearance choices?
    a. Tattoos and piercings are acceptable to all generations.
    b. Dressing for yourself surpasses dressing for the customer.
    c. Your appearance speaks volumes—both positive and negative—to your customers.
    d. Call center employees needn't worry about appearance.

4. Which of the following contributes most to going the "extra mile"?
    a. Arriving at work on time
    b. Taking your lunch break on time
    c. Regularly confirming your empowerment options with your supervisor
    d. Understanding what others do before you and after you in the workflow

5. In face-to-face interactions, using the "10 feet—5 feet" rule for greeting is recommended.
    a. True
    b. False

6. When serving your customers, which of following is recommended?
    a. Keep promises you make.
    b. Be extraordinary—exceeding customer expectations.
    c. Use caution to not smother your customers.
    d. Create the customer's desire to return.
    e. All of the above

7. Virtually all buildings are ADA-compliant, so customers' special needs are not pertinent to the overall customer experience?
    a. True
    b. False

8. When interacting with a customer who is in a wheelchair or transport chair, which of the following is not appropriate?
    a. Bend over or kneel when speaking with the customer.
    b. Interact with the customer as you would any other customer.
    c. Speak to and not at the person.
    d. Don't touch the wheelchair or transport chair without the customer's permission.

9. Which of the following are cues to quickly identify a customer's behavior?
   a. Outgoing and rigid
   b. Outgoing and flexible
   c. Reserved and rigid
   d. Reserved and flexible
   e. All of the above
   f. None of the above

10. Which of the following would we prefer as customers?
   a. Commander
   b. Concentrator
   c. Cooperator
   d. None of the above

11. Which of the following should you not do when interacting with a "commander"?
   a. Move to a secluded location if possible.
   b. Tell the customer to lower their voice.
   c. Let the customer talk themselves out.
   d. Over-apologize—even if you have done nothing wrong.

12. Which of the following is a positive way to interact with a "cooperator"?
   a. Engage in active listening.
   b. Work to build a relationship.
   c. Acknowledge the "cooperator's" understanding.
   d. Work in partnership for the highest level of a win-win outcome.
   e. All of the above
   f. None of the above

13. Aggressively confronting people leads to solutions.
    a. True
    b. False

14. All components of the service-recovery template must be used when dealing with an unhappy customer.
    a. True
    b. False

15. James was working with a customer to resolve a service issue when the customer began shouting profanities and threatening him. James should do which of the following?
    a. Accept that some people are easily upset and communicate through it.
    b. Remind the customer that they are the cause of the problem.
    c. Let the customer know he is terminating the proceedings.
    d. Let the customer continue until the customer is calmer.

16. Under which of the following conditions should you escalate a customer issue?
    a. The request exceeds the Customer Service Professional's authority.
    b. The customer demands to speak with a supervisor.
    c. The customer threatens legal action against the company.
    d. The customer engages in threatening behavior.
    e. All of the above
    f. None of the above

17. Customers can influence your organization's strategic direction.
    a. True
    b. False

18. Which of the following phrases is not appropriate to use when closing a customer interaction?
    a. "Thank you."
    b. "No problem."
    c. "Please come again."
    d. "It's my pleasure."
    e. All of the above

19. Which of the following is not a component of service recovery?
    a. Apologizing
    b. Offering alternatives
    c. Treating customers based on their attitude
    d. Actively listening
    e. None of the above

20. The Rotary International's self-assessment tool that can help Customer Service Professionals build long-lasting customer loyalty is called the "Three-Way Test."
    a. True
    b. False

CHAPTER 6

Effective Email Communication

Many Customer Service Professionals deal with their customers via email as a primary form of communication—either initially or in follow-up. Regardless of why email communication is employed, it is important that the Customer Service Professional fully understand how to use it correctly.

Our skills in developing a formal business communication document have waned over time, as email has taken over as a preferred messaging approach. And email has itself become more casual—possibly a bit too casual. To maintain an assured professional tone in all of your business writings, you should consider email just a different form of letter writing and adjust your use accordingly. There are occasions when informal emails are acceptable, and there are times when they are not. Your job is to assure you always know and incorporate the right tone in all communications.

Let's explore the components and effective use of emailing in detail.

When Email Should Be Employed

Email is an appropriate communication medium when:

- An immediate response is not important. People have different approaches to when they check and respond to email, and their timing might not meet your expectation for an urgent response, so always consider the emergent nature of the notice or needed response.
- Geography or scheduling makes it particularly challenging to interact face-to-face—whether in-person or virtual—or by telephone. If you are communicating with customers in different time zones, email accommodates all schedules more effectively.
- The message is appropriate for a generic audience, and confidentiality is not an issue. In this case, email is a quick way to deliver the message.
- Written evidence of the communication is required.

When Email Should Not Be Employed

Email communication should not be used when:

- The message has an unusually large volume of detail—then another means of communicating should be employed. People tend to shy away from reading long, intense emails. You may want to create a shared file that your intended recipient(s) can access at their convenience, versus recreating the information in an email, which isn't as conducive to manipulating, sorting the data, etc.
- The sender has an emotional issue—angry, sad, distracted. An email should not be written or sent at this time. Doing so can result in unwanted consequences for the sender and possibly the organization.

- You do not have time to prepare a thoughtful, complete message. Rushing will lead to recipient confusion and follow-up to clarify the original email. Time is wasted and that is a limited commodity.
- You are unsure whether an email could create legal exposure for you or your organization. And if you like to "vent" in an email to yourself but not send it to anyone, keep in mind that it is discoverable under many legal searches. Find another way to vent.
- The information is personal or confidential and could create controversy if shared inappropriately. Always ask yourself, if this content were published in the local newspaper, would that be OK? If the answer is "no," don't write it.

Email Preparation

Emails should be treated as if they are a professional business communication—because they are. While some of the following information may appear obvious, it is important to apply to emailing.

All emails should have a defined structure. Diagram 6-1 provides the structural components of an effective email.

EMAIL STRUCTURAL COMPONENTS

- Date—provided automatically by email applications
- To—recipient name(s). Always double-check that you are sending to the people you intended and that you limit blind copying as much as possible.
- Subject—the purpose of the email—be clear. Try to limit your email to one topic.
- Salutation—your opening greeting. Always open with a greeting: "Hello," "Hi," "Good day," etc.
- Body—the main part of the email. A couple of paragraphs maximum is the goal if you want it read and responded to quickly.

- Call for Action—what is expected of the email recipient(s). Either start or end with what specifically you need, e.g., a response or report by a particular date, or confirmation of the next meeting.
- Closing—Sign off with sender information. You can easily set up a signature line with whatever details you want recipients to have.

SAMPLE EMAIL FORMAT

- **Your Name and Email Address**
  (Provided by Email Application)
- **Today's Date**
  (Provided by Email Application)
- **Recipient(s) —"To"; "Cc"; "Bcc"**
- **Subject**
- **Attach Files as Necessary**
- **Salutation**
- **Body of Email**
  - Length
  - Topic
  - Context
  - Format
  - Tone
  - Words
- **Call for Action**
- **Closing**
  - Include sender's contact information

DIAGRAM 6-1

FOCUSED EMAILS

The most effective emails address a **single topic.** This allows the recipient to focus on just that subject and increases the likelihood of a response in less time. As an additional benefit, it allows both the sender and receiver to file the email by topic.

EMAIL RECIPIENTS

There are three options for email recipients: "To" [primary recipient(s)], "Cc" (carbon copy) and "Bcc" (blind carbon copy).

"To" Field Considerations

Include recipients in the "To" field if:

- The email recipient expects you to provide information.
- You expect action or information from the recipient.
- You feel the information will or may be useful to the recipient.
- Sending information to the recipients needs to be recorded for legal reasons.

Examples include:

- You committed to get the updated refund policy to a customer.
- You need a customer to provide you with product registration information.
- You want your supervisor to be aware of a system outage in the Deerfield, Connecticut, office.

"Cc" Field Considerations

Include recipients in the "Cc" field if:

- The information will or may be useful to the recipient, but they are not required to take subsequent action.
- You want to create an added sense of authority. Occasionally it is appropriate to "cc" someone in a position of authority to assure other recipients you have that individual's support.

Examples include:

- You are going on vacation next week and send an email to your co-workers sharing your plans and copy your supervisor as a reminder.
- You are having difficulty getting a response from the recipient, and you copy your supervisor—consider this as a last resort.

"Bcc" Field Considerations

- Use "Bcc" on an extremely limited, exception-only basis.
- Unlike "To" or "Cc," "Bcc" email recipients do not see each other's names or email addresses.
- To "blind" all recipients, ensure yours is the only email address in the "To" field. This is appropriate if recipients have no need for or right to the email addresses of other recipients.
- A word of caution. A "Bcc" recipient may inadvertently share their name and email address with those on the "To" and "Cc" list by using a "Reply all" response to the email. What you had intended as a confidential recipient is then known by many.

Examples include:

- You want to send an email to your customer base and do not want customers to see each other's names or email information. You add all recipients to the "Bcc" field and create an email address with a name such as "To Our Valued Customers" for the "To" field.
- You are having difficulty working with a particular customer. You may "Bcc" your supervisor to ensure they are aware of the message content and timing.

INTELLIGENT SUBJECT LINES

You should treat your email subject line as if it were a newspaper headline. It should be intelligent— providing clarity regarding the main point of the email. It could contain instructional information, such as "Customer Contract Copy Attached" or "Immediate Attention Required."

You can make the subject line the entire email by entering "EOM" (end of message) at the end of the subject line. For example, an email subject line might say, "Reminder—Blood Drive Today in Conference Room A 9:00 a.m. to 4:00 p.m. (EOM)."

If you receive an email that contains more than one topic and your response does not address all the topics, you should edit the subject line to reflect your response. This is helpful when you want to find a particular email by subject.

Poor Subject Lines
- Entirely blank, containing no information
- "Meeting"—when? Where?
- "Update"—on what?
- "Follow-Up"—on what?
- "Fw: Fw: Fw: Fw: This Thursday"—limit to a single "Fw"
- "See Me"—when? Why?

Rich Subject Lines
- "Updated Online Ordering Forms"
- "Thursday Call Agenda"
- "Reminder—Email Server Down 3–5 p.m. 5/17/22 (EOM)"

SALUTATION

Your salutation clarifies for whom the email is intended. If you ever received an email and couldn't discern if you were the planned recipient, you are not alone. Ensuring your emails have a clear salutation removes all doubt for the email recipients.

The **less** familiar you are with the recipient(s) and the more **formal** the email, the more formal should be your salutation. When in doubt, address the recipient(s) more formally to avoid offending them.

Salutation examples—less formal to more formal:
a. "Latisha"
b. "Dear Robert"
c. "Dear Ms. Johnson"

If you do not know the recipient's name, use a generic salutation:
a. "Good morning, everyone"
b. "To Our Valued Customers"
c. "Memorandum to Representatives of the Service Promotion Team"

BODY

The body of your **email is the critical component**—ensure that the message you intend to share is as clear as it can be. The key components and considerations in creating an effective email body are:
a. Length
b. Topic
c. Context
d. Format
e. Tone
f. Words

Length. Think through the bottom-line message you want to convey. The more complex the message, the more time it takes to write it in order to keep it reasonably brief. You may need to write a draft or two before you reach a satisfactory final document. Remember, brevity is an asset.

Topic. Often, we need to communicate with recipients regarding a number of different topics. The recipient(s) may be able to respond quickly to one of the topics, while requiring additional research time before responding to other topics—which means the easy response is delayed while the recipient considers how to respond to the more complex items. Again, recipients are more likely to read and act upon emails if they address a single topic—which is ideal.

Context. Context is the background, environment, framework or situation surrounding your topic. It is necessary so the recipient can more effectively understand and respond—if required—to your email. For example, "Please provide the ABC report" provides no context for the requested information. However, "We are in receipt of your invoice and supporting documents for the Customer Service Center Expansion Project. In order to process this payment, we require a completed ABC report. Once received, we can proceed with processing your payment."

With the language used in the second email, the recipient has additional information that indicates the "why" of the request. Thus, there is context for the recipient, and you are far more likely to get what you need.

Formatting. Email messages must be easy to navigate. When setting up your email formatting, ensure the recipients don't lose the intent of the email due to distracting elements. Research suggests the following in your email formatting:

- Avoid distracting backgrounds or wallpaper.
- Use simple fonts such as Arial, Times New Roman and Calibri.
- Do not use more than two fonts within the email.
- Use a type size that is easy to read. Typically, 10– or 11-point type size makes for comfortable reading.
- You may use color to highlight a key point; however, too many colors are distracting.
- Use paragraphs to separate thoughts. The white space between paragraphs makes the email much easier to read. Always avoid run-on writing.
- Bullets or numbered lists can make details easier to identify.
- Write in complete sentences.
- Use bold type sparingly—only to highlight critical or essential information. Don't "shout" at people by overusing bold type.

Tone. How do you know the intended tone of an email? In face-to-face, virtual and phone communication, you have nonverbals, volume and rate of speech to help you identify the tone of the interaction. While you lack these important communication cues with email, you can use verbiage to indicate your intended tone.

You can set the email's tone in the opening line.
- "I enjoyed our meeting last Thursday."
- "I hope your week is going well."
- "I appreciate your contributions on the customer feedback project."

- "I am disappointed in your lack of response to my request."
- "I am at my wits' end!"

We would likely view the first three messages positively at the outset. The last two suggest an unhappy sender. All, though, add some important context to the email. Remember, setting the proper tone can help manage the reader's understanding of your intended message and delivering on your expectations.

Words. When selecting the words you use in your email, it is important to consider the language skills of your audience.

- Do not use terminology that your customer may not typically use. What may seem common and easy for you may not translate well by the customer.
- Always use proper grammar as well as spelling, capitalization and punctuation.
- Remember the respectful basics of "please" and "thank you."
- Spell out acronyms the first time you use them in an email, such as "Customer Retention Report—(CRR)." Put "CRR" in parentheses following the full name of the report so that the customer will connect the two when seeing the acronym elsewhere in the email. After initially spelled out, acronyms may be used in the remainder of the email.
- Avoid informal abbreviations and acronyms such as "btw" (by the way), "eod" (end of day) and "b/c" (because).
- Use emoticons very sparingly and never in **formal** emails.

Remember, the more formal the email, the more formal the language the sender should employ.

CALL FOR ACTION

Too often, our emails are unclear regarding what we expect of the recipients—if anything.

If an email is an "FYI" (for your information), clarify this up front to the recipient:

- Example: "This email is for your information only and no formal response is required."

If the email requires an action of the recipient, specify exactly what you are requesting:

- Example: "Please provide your address and phone number no later than Wednesday at noon."

The call for action may come at the beginning or the end of the email, or both (for emphasis).

- Example: "I will call you on Thursday to discuss the content of this email."

The key here is to never be vague or unclear regarding what you expect from the email recipient. Otherwise, you may receive incorrect or incomplete information, thus creating more work for you and the recipient.

CLOSING

As with the greeting, the less familiar you are with the recipient(s) and the more formal the email, the more formal your closing. Again, if you have any doubt, always choose a more formal closing.

Closing examples—less formal to more formal:
a. "Mary"
b. "Thanks, Samantha"
c. "Best regards, David"
d. "Sincerely, Gale Jones"

The sender's contact information should be provided after the closing. This should include title, organization and phone number(s). This will make it easier for the recipient(s) to contact you in various ways as needed. Use caution if adding quotations below your email closing—such as, "If you think you can or you think you can't—you are right." Some organizations may have a policy concerning this practice, so check with your organization's leadership regarding any requirements you must follow. Currently, there is much discussion whether religious quotations can or should be used after email closings. If there is doubt as to whether a quotation may offend your customers, we suggest you avoid it.

Some organizations require a legal disclaimer on all outgoing emails. You should comply with your organization's disclaimer policy.

> *The benefit of a well-constructed email far surpasses the time required to do so.*
> —C. WILLIAM CRUTCHER

Email Legal Considerations

Emails maintain the same legal standing as other forms of business correspondence—even emails you send to yourself or that sit in your "drafts" folder. They are official business records and, as such, are discoverable in legal proceedings. (This is another good reason to create professionally structured emails.) Grand juries can subpoena not only the person who created a document, but any third parties who might be in possession of that document. Additionally, "deleted" emails are often recoverable given system backups and current technology, so operate from the premise that an email is never deleted.

Do not include language in an email that may be misconstrued in any manner as illegal discrimination. For example, unless something is a BFOQ (bona fide occupational qualification), you may not include any reference that could be viewed as discriminatory in your hiring practices.

Email Missteps

Not following email structure guidelines and taking shortcuts in any of the above steps will just lead to more work for you. You should avoid the following:

100

- Overusing email when not necessary—when a phone call, face-to-face or virtual meeting would be equally or more effective. A good guideline to follow: If you have had four important substantive exchanges by email, pick up the phone.
- Failing to verify email addresses—results in unnecessary returned emails and additional time to obtain the correct information.
- Assuming deleting an email removes the "paper trail"—which it definitely does not.
- Disregarding the potential consequences of sending copyrighted material—can create legal exposure for you and your organization.
- Ignoring emails that require action—sending a response like, "I am currently unable to respond fully to your email, but will do so by this Thursday" is better than leaving the sender wondering if you received their email.
- Not setting up an automatic reply when you are out of the office. Always include in your auto reply when you will return and who is in charge of your area while you are gone.
- Sending an "urgent" email expecting an immediate reply—in-person or telephone contact is optimal when something is needed right away.
- Assuming recipients fully understand your company's inner workings—hierarchy, processes, systems, jargon—leading to ineffective email communication.

In closing, whether you are using email as a primary form of communication or only occasionally, it is important to recognize the need to create professional, effective emails. Doing so can ensure that the message you intended to send is the one the recipients actually received. Effective email plays a pivotal role in your organization's success and simplifies your life.

Chapter Review Questions

1. In which of the following situations is an email acceptable?
   a. David needs immediate assistance with a customer issue.
   b. Latoya is in a rush and asking Bob for input on a challenging project.
   c. Richard needs written confirmation of information he is sending to a customer.
   d. Monica wants to share her personal insights about Linda with her boss.

2. Email is a speedy and effective means to vent your feelings on an issue.
   a. True
   b. False

3. Which of the following does a formal email not need to contain?
   a. Salutation
   b. Subject
   c. Body
   d. Response due date

4. A focused email is one that:
   a. Is sent to only one receiver
   b. Involves a single topic
   c. Provides in-depth detail
   d. Requires immediate action

5. You should include recipients in the email "To" field if:
   a. You want to create an increased sense of authority.
   b. The email recipient(s) might be interested in the subject.
   c. You are having difficulty getting the recipient to respond to you.
   d. You need action or information from the recipient.

6. Include a recipient in the email "Cc" field if you feel the information will be useful to them but they are not required to take subsequent action.
   a. True
   b. False

7. What is the best means to "blind" all recipients on an email?
   a. Include a disclaimer that the email content may not be shared without written permission.
   b. Send individual emails to all recipients.
   c. Include all email addresses in the "Bcc" field.
   d. None of the above

8. An email subject line should be brief and to the point.
   a. True
   b. False

9. "EOM" at the end of an email subject line indicates "edit or modify" content.
   a. True
   b. False

10. Which of the following is not a component of the "body" of an email?
    a. Defined acronyms
    b. Format
    c. Tone
    d. Topic

11. Effective email formatting includes which of the following?
    a. Simple fonts
    b. Complete sentences
    c. Limited color for highlighting only
    d. Paragraphing—avoiding run-on writing
    e. All of the above
    f. None of the above

12. Though an email may contain only words, numbers and characters, there are ways to provide the intended "tone" of the email.
    a. True
    b. False

13. Which of the following ignores the language skills of your audience?
    a. Using terminology that is potentially beyond the customer's understanding
    b. Avoiding respectful basics such as "please" and "thank you"
    c. Including abbreviations such as "eod" (end of day)
    d. Employing emoticons to shorten email content
    e. All of the above
    f. None of the above

14. Emails do not maintain the same legal standing as do a company's formally prepared documents.
    a. True
    b. False

15. Which of the following can undermine effective email communication?
    a. Using email too frequently when a phone call or in-person meeting is warranted
    b. Ignoring professional email structure guidelines
    c. Believing that erasing an email removes the "paper trail"
    d. Sending an urgent email expecting an immediate reply
    e. Ignoring an email that requires your action
    f. All of the above
    g. None of the above

16. As a "Bcc" recipient in email communication, selecting "Reply All" will only respond to the sender, and not the recipients in the "To" and "Cc" fields.
    a. True
    b. False

CHAPTER 7

Appreciating the Impact of Stress

Stress impacts all of us—in varying ways and to varying degrees. Not addressing the stress in your life can result in serious consequences for you and for others around you—including your customers. And stress is cumulative—until you deal with a particular stress-creating issue, that stress remains in your life. Only through resolution can you reduce the negative consequences of stressful events.

Defining stress:

- **Stress is the human reaction to any situation, good or bad, that causes us to readjust.**
- **Stress is what you experience when you believe you cannot effectively cope with a threatening situation.**

Types of Stress

- **Physical**—caused by external and internal factors
- **Social**—caused by interactions between an individual and their environment

- **Psychological**—strong emotions brought on by external or internal factors

GOOD STRESS

Not all stress is harmful to us. Examples of good stressors include:
- Getting the job you wanted
- Getting engaged to be married
- Winning the lottery

BAD STRESS

This is the type of stress with which we are most familiar and can definitely be detrimental to us. Examples of bad stressors include:
- A challenging work environment
- Overwhelming sights and sounds
- Threat of personal injury
- Health issues
- Loss of any sort

Stress Triggers—Causes of Stress

Stress doesn't just hide around the corner, waiting to pounce on you when you pass by. Certain situations—which vary for each of us—cause us to experience stress.

WORK-RELATED STRESS

There are many circumstances on the job that can lead to increased stress levels. These stressors can range from marginal to significantly impacting your well-being.

Deadlines. Most of us have been faced with a work, school or project deadline. The closer the deadline approaches, the more the assignment weighs on us. This can be particularly stressful for procrastinators—deceiving yourself into thinking you can wait to begin the assignment, only finding yourself rushing to finish and then being concerned about the quality of the product—more stress!

Time Limitations. For many people, the constant pursuit to meet and often exceed the needs of customers, co-workers, leadership, family and oneself can be a bit overwhelming. The paradoxical challenge is that we all want more time, yet we have all the time that exists. So more time cannot be the solution. Better use of the time we have is the only answer.

Inability to Say "No." Some people have a difficult time saying "no" to any request. That openness to always serve, no matter what, can place them in the non-envied role of the "go-to" person—that co-worker, volunteer or family member who everyone knows will take on any given task. Might this "yes" person have esteem issues, a high need for achievement or other internal or external driving forces? Whatever the motivation to please or serve, they are causing themselves even greater stress by accepting any opportunity that comes their way and then forcing themselves to do it perfectly.

Work-Life Balance. A major struggle for most of us is maintaining a positive work-life balance. Because of a variety of factors, we find ourselves working more hours and having less free time to enjoy our non-work interests. The constant struggle to balance our home and work lives can be a very real source of stress.

I recall one occasion when we were instructing a stress-management class for a company. When the discussion turned to work-life balance, the participants became quite vocal. They reported to a vice president who required them to work an inordinate amount of overtime. One of them shared that after work one Friday, this executive called them all back to the office, and they ended up working the entire weekend on a project that they all agreed really wasn't urgent. At the crux of the problem was that the employees were actually afraid of the vice president. I could feel their collective stress in that room.

It is up to us to find ways to balance time for work and time for self and others. Sometimes, whether we like it or not, we tolerate longer hours on the job because we feel we do not have an alternative. The truth is there are always alternatives. A more powerful truth is that not finding and engaging these alternatives can have negative consequences for us, our families and those around us.

Leadership. As indicated in the example above, leadership influences our overall stress levels. Does your supervisor treat you and other employees fairly and respectfully? Are performance evaluations constructive? Do you work with or for your supervisor? The dynamics associated with supervisory relationships are a definite source of workplace stress. The results of a poor employee-supervisor relationship can have us coming to work on Monday looking forward to Friday! Wishing away five-sevenths of your life is a sorry situation.

Co-workers. The people you work with can be a source of stress. When cliques exist and we are not a part of them, we can feel ostracized—like we do not matter. It is not unusual in such groups to find an informal leader who has a high need for power—causing others to do what they may not otherwise do. Other members of the group may tolerate this behavior to prevent being banished by the "leader." The best way to handle cliques is to not join them and to not play into their desired influence. They typically don't display the values most of us expect from others, and it will not be a personal loss for you. Instead, create relationships with those who are more like you in maturity and personal values.

Bullying. Another source of co-worker stress is exposure to a bully. Bullies are typically insecure and engage in these behaviors to feel important. Bullying behavior should never be tolerated. When it is, it is to the detriment of those working with or near the person. We recommend that if you are bullied, you engage this individual in a one-on-one conversation. Use some of the techniques for dealing with a "commander" we discussed in Chapter 5.

Compassion Fatigue. Constant concern with caring about and helping others can be draining and mentally exhausting. This is particularly common in "helping" professions and can certainly exist in any customer service setting. It can be incredibly stressful to always be nice, helpful and positive, despite how a customer may actually make you feel or how serious and out of control a situation may be.

Job Burnout. Job burnout can create additional stress, which is often difficult to accurately identify.

Job burnout is not:
- Being very busy—most of us are very busy
- Being at one job too long—we are fortunate when we find a job we enjoy doing for many years
- A result of an occasional work crisis—virtually every job has, at one time or another, some sort of brief calamity

Job burnout is a complex set of problems that can impact your ability to:
- Tolerate emotional demands of the job
- Cope with daily stressors of the workplace
- Muster the enthusiasm to do a job well

*The **signs of job burnout** that you should be aware of include **constantly:***
- Feeling drained and lacking energy—it is a real struggle to get through the day mentally and physically
- Being cynical and mistrusting your organization
- Being short-tempered with co-workers
- Providing poor customer service—not appreciating the real value of customers
- Working through breaks and lunches—unable to appropriately disengage from work
- Suffering muscle, head or body aches and pains
- Being uninspired to laugh—finding no reason to see joy in the workplace

Job burnout is a real phenomenon, and if you are finding it difficult to get up every day and go to work, take advantage of your organization's mental health benefits or employee assistance program (EAP) to assess what you are experiencing and why. Allow yourself the privilege of getting better, re-enjoying your job or moving on with satisfaction.

FAMILY DYNAMICS STRESS

A number of issues within the family dynamic can produce stress for an individual.

Finances. Family finances are common stressors for members of the household. Few people have all the money they desire, and many find it difficult to meet monthly obligations. Worrying about how you will pay the rent or mortgage, put adequate food on the table, or pay accumulated medical or other bills can be, and often is, a major issue for many people. It hangs over us—seemingly always—and until we manage to get our finances under control, can remain a highly stress-inducing issue for us.

Infidelity. When cheating occurs in a relationship, the relationship partners typically exhibit heightened levels of negative stress. We count on our partner being there for us through thick and thin. If they or we violate the vows of this relationship through unfaithfulness, that sanctuary that was our home is negatively impacted. Regardless of its source or rationale, the infidelity creates a significant level of bad stress. Until we deal with repairing the relationship or moving on, the stress remains with us.

Separation or Divorce. Separating or divorcing parties are under overwhelming stress both at home and at work. There is no peace or personal sanctuary, and it shows in all interactions. And the impact of the separation or divorce reaches well beyond the couple. While it is obviously a challenge for the adults, children may find their worlds as they knew them destroyed, and some may feel responsible for the couple's separation. Their stress may impact their ability to interact with others or concentrate on school and homework. Handling a separation or divorce appropriately takes time and commitment by both partners to ensure the impact on children is minimized to the extent possible.

Human Loss. Another source of family-sourced stress is the loss of a loved one. The length of time we need to accept the loss depends on the physical, intellectual and emotional tie we had with the loved one who has passed. The stronger the bond, the greater the stress and the longer it takes to accept the loss.

Take, for example, a young lady who loses her grandmother. Let's view this from two perspectives. In the first situation, the young lady lived several states away and her only contact with her grandmother was receiving an annual birthday card. In the second situation, the young lady was raised by her grandmother and thus, the grandmother was her mother figure. As we might expect, the stress caused by the loss of the grandmother in the first case is far less than the stress felt in the second case. In either situation, there is really nothing to "fix"—only time can heal and reduce the related stress, and professional counseling may help during this healing time.

LIFE STRESS

Life in general can be a cause of stress for us, from a number of sources. Obviously, we all have different life experiences and issues. Following are some of the more common life sources of stress.

Personal Health. The overall state of our health can be a source of added stress. Stress can negatively impact our muscles, heart, circulatory and immune systems. When we are in great shape—physically, mentally and emotionally—we typically approach people and situations more positively overall. If we are dealing with challenging health issues, stress is often an unwanted companion. Even just "not feeling good" can be enough to interfere with our day-to-day activities, including our valued relationships. A more serious ailment can be even more devastating to you and those around you. Thus, it is important to strongly consider engaging in activities that support good physical and mental health. As we discussed earlier, this requires a clear attitude of personal wellness for long-term success.

Body Image. What do we think about our personal appearance? Feeling we look good contributes to good stress and can raise our confidence in how we handle ourselves in various situations. However, a negative body image can lead to extremely elevated levels of bad stress. Even though our appearance may look fine to others, when we do not see ourselves in the same light, we may engage in activities that are detrimental to our overall health. Professionals in this field can help us reduce the stress associated with a poor personal body image.

Addictions. Sadly, too many people experience harmful compulsions. These can be a significant source of stress that impacts us and those around us. I shared earlier my addiction to tobacco. By adopting a strong negative attitude toward smoking, I was able to successfully control the addiction. Until I was able to do so, trying or wanting to quit was quite stressful for me and those close to me. Obviously, there are many other addictions that are harmful to us physically, mentally and emotionally. These may include—but are not limited to—alcohol, drugs and gambling, and can even include being a "workaholic." Any addiction that contributes to bad stress is harmful to you and those who care for you. Individuals with addictions typically require professional help and support for long-term recovery for themselves and those close to them.

Rules and Regulations. Another cause for stress can be all the rules, policies and laws we are required to follow. Rules exist to protect us and others—including our customers. These rules can be long-term or temporary. For example, we all understand the need to stop at a red light, so this is rarely a source of stress—unless we are late for something. For many individuals, the feeling of being constrained by rules can be a source of stress—especially when we view them as working against us. This may be a "control" issue for us, and we may need assistance in finding ways of letting go. Accepting and truly appreciating the reasons for rules and regulations can help reduce this stress.

The World. Overall global conditions can have an impact on our stress levels. How we view current external conditions—wherever they may occur in the world—directly influences our stress levels, both good and bad. Some situations are more important to us than others, and could include a variety of issues, from the standings of our favorite sports teams to economic markets, political situations and even general weather conditions. And with social media, we receive information—both true and untrue—about worldly happenings constantly and currently. It is important that we find coping mechanisms that work for us when we feel our world just isn't working for us.

Stress Reduction Tools and Techniques

There are many ways to reduce stress. Some are immediate; others take more time, but all require that you acknowledge the stress and deal with it in some fashion that suits you and adequately addresses the level and type of stress you are experiencing. Eventually, you will want to focus on maintaining a stress-resilient mindset. You will learn how to set values, goals and attitudes that contribute to a consistently positive state of mind.

Effective stress management means more than having the right stress-reducing tools and techniques—it means knowing how to balance the pressure and demands in your life—and doing so with personal satisfaction, pleasure and a lifestyle that significantly insulates you from the negative impact of stress.

Your lifestyle can significantly impact how much stress you feel on a daily basis. It is important to engage in stress-reduction activities as much as possible. Here are some positive examples to consider.

- Find your "sanctuary"—that place to which you can escape, without stress-related issues.
- Take a bath—sitting in a warm tub can help soothe the soul as well as the body.
- Take a walk—find a tranquil place, and reflect on what is good in your life.
- Talk to a friend—someone who is not judgmental and genuinely cares about your well-being.
- Read a book—allow yourself to mentally "check out" of your current reality for a while.
- Join a group you find to be a positive contributor to good stress.
- Get a pet—often animals can provide emotional support and offer wonderful stress reduction.
- Get out of the house—do anything!
- Live according to your values, without regret.
- Find a reason to laugh every day!

- Take a few minutes to give yourself some positive coaching, focusing on good things about yourself, those around you and your job.
- Practice appreciation, simply by acknowledging anything and anyone in your life for which you are grateful—it's a fantastic way to shift into a better mindset. It is helpful to write these down so you can look at the list occasionally as a reminder of the positive things in your life.
- Take opportunities to let those for whom you are grateful know what they mean to you.
- And finally, concern yourself with only what is important as well as what **you** can control.

In summary, both good and bad stress exist in our lives. It is extremely important to find ways to recognize and appreciate the good stress and avoid, or effectively address, contributors to the bad stress. When we are able to manage our stress more successfully, we are better equipped to serve the needs of others—especially our customers.

> *The greatest weapon against stress is our ability*
> *to choose one thought over another.*
> —WILLIAM JAMES

Chapter Review Questions

1. Which of the following is not a type of stress?
    a. Psychological
    b. Aggressive
    c. Physical
    d. Social

2. Stress occurs when you feel you cannot effectively cope with a threatening situation.
    a. True
    b. False

3. Which of the following is not a trigger for good stress?
    a. A challenging work environment
    b. Winning a new car in a raffle drawing
    c. Getting a much-wanted promotion
    d. Relaxing at the beach
    e. All of the above

4. Most stressful situations are the same for the majority of people.
    a. True
    b. False

5. Which of the following represents a work-related stress trigger?
    a. Having a bully as a co-worker
    b. Inability to say "No" to requests
    c. Uneven balance between work and personal time
    d. Disrespectful supervisor
    e. All of the above
    f. None of the above

6. Not having some form of "sanctuary" can contribute to overall stress levels.
   a. True
   b. False

7. "Compassion fatigue" refers to which of the following?
   a. Being treated unfairly by a supervisor
   b. Always being the go-to problem-solver
   c. Constant concern associated with caring about and helping others
   d. Being empathetic toward co-workers
   e. All of the above
   f. None of the above

8. Which of the following is a significant source of family stress?
   a. Loss of a loved one
   b. Infidelity
   c. Finances
   d. Divorce or separation
   e. All of the above

9. When experiencing the loss of a loved one, time is often the best healer.
   a. True
   b. False

10. Which of the following is a "life" source of bad stress?
    a. Feeling healthy and fit
    b. Addiction of any kind
    c. Accepting rules that must be followed
    d. Positive personal body image
    e. All of the above

11. Luckily for us, all stress just dissipates over time.
    a. True
    b. False

12. Which of the following is an example of an effective stress reducer?
    a. Finding your "sanctuary"
    b. Taking a walk
    c. Reading a book
    d. Living according to your values
    e. All of the above

13. We are fortunate that events in other countries do not impact our overall stress levels.
    a. True
    b. False

14. Which of the following is not a sign of job burnout?
    a. Being short-tempered with customers
    b. Feeling drained and lacking overall energy
    c. Not appreciating the real value of customers
    d. Being very busy
    e. All of the above

15. A good stress reduction technique is to recognize that while we cannot prevent all stress, we should concern ourselves with only what is important, as well as what we can control, or at minimum influence.
    a. True
    b. False

CHAPTER 8

Sexual Harassment—Principles and Prevention

Defining sexual harassment can be challenging because it is determined by the perception of the person who feels sexually harassed. What is perceived as an innocent glance by one person might be a suggestive leer to another. But the intent of the look is less relevant than its effect. If the recipient feels uncomfortable, they can deem the behavior harassing and take legal action.

What behaviors are considered sexual harassment? In summary, they include:

- Unwelcome sexual advances in any form
- Unwelcome requests for sexual favors
- Other unwelcome verbal or physical conduct of a sexual nature

Legal Definition

The courts define sexual harassment as **"Unwelcome sexual advances and requests for special favors or other verbal or physical conduct of a sexual nature."**

Overtly, sexual harassment includes lewd comments, inappropriate physical contact, or requests for sexual favors in return for job security or career advancement. But sexual harassment is often subtler. For example, an employee may enjoy complimenting their co-workers' appearance. Another might think telling off-color jokes is fun and encourages camaraderie. But such behavior can be legally defined as sexual harassment. If someone complains, your opinion about the intention is irrelevant. You may think the compliments are innocent or the jokes are harmless, but if someone else perceives them as a problem, they are a problem.

Sexual Harassment and the Law

Sexual harassment law finds its roots in Title VII of the Civil Rights Act of 1964 and subsequent amendments. While this act applies nationally to companies with more than 15 employees, it is important to check your state law, as it may reduce this number to as low as **one employee.**

Title VII prohibits discrimination on the basis of race, color, religion, national origin, and gender. Since 1964, numerous Title VII–related cases have continued to refine the definition of acts that represent sexual harassment. The Civil Rights Act of 1991 provided for the inclusion of jury trials and increased damages in Title VII cases.

Simple Guideline

Is it or isn't it sexual harassment? Because determining whether an action constitutes sexual harassment is often a challenge, consider abiding by the following guideline:

If it is unwanted and sexual in nature, it IS sexual harassment.

While the intention may be honorable, it is the perception that matters. If you are not sure, then DON'T! It is that simple. No harassment of any type **is** the law.

Why People Engage in Sexually Harassing Conduct

Multiple theories exist about why people engage in sexually harassing behavior. Among the most common are:
- A strong dislike of an individual for their sexual orientation
- Predatory orientation toward others
- Desire to gain feelings of power by threatening, bullying and sexually harassing others
- Ignorance of the law—not understanding what constitutes sexual harassment
- "Old habits"—not recognizing that the law and social norms have appropriately advanced

Importance of Sexual Harassment Training

No one wants to wake up in the morning and read a newspaper headline indicating they or their organization are involved in a sexual harassment claim. To reduce this likelihood, it is imperative that ALL employees be trained on sexual harassment and prevention principles. This is important because:

- Sexual harassment is illegal in every form.
- There is growing sensitivity to the issue and a much stronger likelihood of someone acting on their rights to be treated respectfully and lawfully.
- There are many forms of sexual harassment, and some may not be as obvious.
- Training clarifies reporting procedures for employees should there be a potential sexual harassment incident.
- It contributes to a more positive, productive and respectful work environment—one that is appreciated and enjoyed by all customers.

Sexual Harassment Categories

There are two categories of sexual harassment: "quid pro quo" and "hostile environment." Let's explore each of these.

QUID PRO QUO SEXUAL HARASSMENT

The straightforward definition of quid pro quo is "one thing in return for another," sometimes described as "this for that." Quid pro quo sexual harassment occurs when an employee is confronted with sexual demands in return for some benefit, such as a raise, a promotion or even keeping their job. The request may be either explicit, such as "If you spend Friday night with me, you'll get a significant cash bonus and that raise you have been asking for," or implicit, such as "People who are cooperative get better performance reviews."

In quid pro quo sexual harassment, the harasser uses submission to or rejection of unwelcome sexual advances or conduct as the basis for employment decisions such as promotions, discharges, transfers, training, salary increases, work assignment or overtime. It is important to note that you don't have to be the direct target of the abuse to be a victim of quid pro quo sexual harassment. An employee can file a harassment claim, for example, if they are passed over for a promotion given to a less qualified co-worker who is allegedly having an affair with the manager.

It only takes **one incident** to get in some profoundly serious trouble. A single—just one—sexual advance can lead to a lawsuit if it is linked to some form of quid pro quo.

Real-Life Example of Quid Pro Quo Sexual Harassment

A manager warned an employee that her continued employment depended on her willingness to have a sexual relationship with him. After meeting him in motels for more than a year, she suddenly ended the affair. Shortly afterwards, her performance appraisal levels were reduced and she was fired. When she sued for sexual harassment, the company argued that it knew nothing about the affair. It also pointed out that no one forced her to go to the hotel with the manager.

In a landmark U.S. Supreme Court decision, the employee's claim of sexual harassment was upheld. The Court ruled that the company should have been aware of the manager's conduct. It also dismissed the company's argument that she was a willing participant in the affair because it was made clear that her job status depended on her cooperation. According to the Court, the fact that she was fired after ending the affair proved quid pro quo sexual harassment (*Meritor Savings Bank v. Vinson*).

HOSTILE ENVIRONMENT SEXUAL HARASSMENT

A sexually hostile environment occurs when unwelcome conduct of a sexual nature unreasonably interferes with an individual's job performance or creates a hostile, intimidating or offensive work environment.

Here are some examples of inappropriate behavior that have created hostile work environments:

- Sexual jokes, anecdotes or remarks
- Sexual cartoons, posters or other graphics
- Sexual intimations or suggestive looks

A victim doesn't have to actually suffer a tangible economic or health injury to build a legal case for hostile work environment sexual harassment. For example, no loss of pay or promotion or deteriorating emotional stability are required. Any unreasonable interference with the victim's work or health is sufficient to claim sexual harassment. Again, it is **perception and not intention** that grounds a sexual harassment complaint. Every complaint must be taken seriously.

Real-Life Examples of Hostile Work Environment Sexual Harassment

Both male and female customer service employees were subjected to harassment by managers as well as co-workers. The hostile environment charges included one manager peering down women's tops to see their breasts and another manager requesting a sexual favor from a female employee. In another occurrence a male worker exposed himself, and there were additional complaints of unwanted touching. The EEOC (Equal Employment Opportunity Commission) also identified a number of male workers subjected to harassment when female co-workers asked them about preferred sexual activities. The EEOC further purported that onsite human resources staff failed to properly address the harassment despite complaints by employees. A settlement of $3.5 million was distributed to the victims. Additionally, the company agreed to a number of preventative safeguards, including sexual harassment training for its employees that contained *civility* and *bystander intervention* instruction (*U.S. EEOC v. Alorica, Inc.*).

In another example of hostile work environment sexual harassment, the victim was harassed but admittedly suffered no loss of pay or promotion. A female employee objected to explicit photos and magazines left in plain view in the workplace. She admitted that she didn't physically suffer any sexual harassment, but she still claimed that sexual harassment had occurred. When the company took no action, she sued, claiming the pornographic material created a hostile work environment. The jury awarded her $875,000 (*Blakey v. Continental Airlines*).

Posting any explicit pornography is clearly over the line, but courts have ruled that even less explicit sexually suggestive images can be just as offensive and, therefore, constitute sexual harassment. Customizing your workspace with pictures, posters, calendars and other personal effects can help you feel more at home, but significant problems can arise if an employee's decorations offend the sensibilities of others.

Hostile work environment behaviors include, but are not limited to:
- Discussing any type of sexual activities
- Telling off-color jokes or stories
- Unnecessary or unwanted touching
- Commenting on physical attributes
- Displaying sexually suggestive images
- Using demeaning or inappropriate terms
- Using indecent gestures
- Using crude or offensive language
- Staring or ogling

Again, it is not the offender's intention, but the perception of the offended person(s) that matters.

Victims of Hostile Work Environment Sexual Harassment

We know that sexual, vulgar or pornographic images, jokes or language can create a hostile environment. But the sexual comments or lewd behavior don't have to be directed at the complainant for them to prove sexual harassment. **Anyone** who is exposed to the inappropriate behavior can claim hostile work environment sexual harassment. Here are some examples:
- A supervisor who sexually harasses an employee may create an intimidating, hostile or offensive work environment for other employees who witness the offending behavior.
- A person who walks into a break room and hears co-workers telling sexually explicit jokes could file a complaint, even though the jokes weren't directed at them.

- Flirting between a supervisor and a willing employee could be perceived as offensive by another employee. This other employee could get the impression that "one has to go along to get along," or could just be uncomfortable with the situation.

Any of these situations could become the basis of a hostile work environment sexual harassment charge.

Topics and Words to Avoid

The following is a quick-reference, non-exhaustive list of behaviors and words to avoid, as each can be perceived as sexual harassment by the offended.

- Jokes with any sexual reference or innuendo
- Words of affection—e.g., "honey," "sweetie," "baby"
- Synonyms for a person—e.g., "chick," "hunk," "stud," "babe"
- References to body parts or bodily functions
- References to sexual preferences, orientation or experiences
- Compliments relative to appearance
- Crude, offensive language
- "Elevator eyes"—looking up and down a person's physique
- Other words or behaviors of a similar nature

Remember, when in doubt . . . DON'T!

Third-Party Sexual Harassment

Employees who work offsite or engage with nonemployees as part of their job are guaranteed protection against sexual harassment by anyone with whom they come in contact on the job—either in person, by phone, virtually or through writing. If supervisors don't take these complaints seriously and investigate immediately, the company can be held responsible for allowing the harassment to occur.

REAL-LIFE EXAMPLE OF THIRD-PARTY SEXUAL HARASSMENT

A female employee was assigned to work on another company's property. She had no employment relationship with the other company and was on its premises only to perform her job. When she complained about sexual harassment, the host company insisted that she leave the premises immediately. Her employer took her off the assignment and, when no suitable alternative work could be found for her, fired her. She sued the company that dismissed her for sexual harassment and retaliation and won her case (*Moland v. Bil-Mar Foods*).

Under the definition of third-party harassment, supervisors are responsible for preventing sexual harassment from anyone over which the company could exercise some control. That includes customers, delivery people, volunteers, suppliers and independent contractors. It is important that you, as a Customer Service Professional, safeguard any third-party individuals in your presence from any type of harassment. That is a positive indicator that both you and your organization take harassment seriously.

Reporting Sexual Harassment

Whether directly involved in or witness to sexual harassment, you are strongly encouraged to take action. Silence may allow the behavior to continue. So, what should you do if you either experience or witness sexual harassment? Here are some guidelines:

- If you are comfortable doing so, let the harasser know you are offended and want the harassing conduct to stop. This may work for a first-time occurrence if you have a reasonably positive relationship with the offender. Your true goal is that the behavior stop.
- Document the sexual harassment (time, date, where, who, what).
- Document your work (keep copies of performance evaluations, disciplinary actions, changes in pay, promotional transfer requests, etc.).

- Identify witnesses or other victims (others who will testify to the facts).
- Use company channels (company policy, grievance procedures)—be aware of your company's policy on harassment—sexual and other.
- File a complaint with the U.S. Office of Equal Employment Opportunity Commission (EEOC) and/or your state's department of human rights. This must be done within 180 days of the last day of the most recent harassment event, based on your best estimate. This may be lengthened to 300 days if the harassment charge is also covered by a state or local anti-discrimination law.

Under current law, the offended individual(s) can charge both the business and the alleged perpetrator in a sexual harassment lawsuit. Characteristically, the business becomes the target because they are assumed to have "deeper pockets"—able to pay larger sums in a settlement. However, when the company can show it took adequate precautions to prevent sexual harassment, such as training all employees, the alleged harasser may become a greater target for the prosecutor and may end up paying financially and professionally.

Remember, if behavior is sexual in nature and is unwelcome, it is sexual harassment, regardless of gender or the offender's intention. It is imperative that employees never engage in such behavior, and if an allegation of sexual harassment does occur, that employees understand both the legal implications and the effects on morale and the business if it is not dealt with appropriately and swiftly. When situations like these make the news, it can have a significant detrimental impact on customer retention.

Bottom line: If you are unsure how a behavior might be perceived by direct or indirect parties, DON'T DO IT!

Chapter Review Questions

1. Which of the following does not constitute sexual harassment?
   a. Unwelcome sexual advances in any form
   b. Requests for sexual favors
   c. Disciplining an employee for poor performance
   d. Verbal or physical conduct of a sexual nature

2. When assessing whether sexual harassment has occurred, the intent of the alleged harasser is often a key factor.
   a. True
   b. False

3. The legal definition of sexual harassment is "Unwelcome sexual advances and requests for special favors or other verbal or physical conduct of a sexual nature."
   a. True
   b. False

4. We can find the foundations of sexual harassment law in which of the following?
   a. Title VII of the Civil Rights Act of 1964
   b. A company's documented policy on sexual harassment
   c. Federal case law of *Griggs v. Alabama*
   d. Occupational Safety and Health Act of 1970

5. What are some of the main reasons people engage in sexually harassing behavior?
    a. Predatory orientation toward others
    b. Strong dislike of an individual for their sexual orientation
    c. Unfamiliarity with the law
    d. All of the above
    e. None of the above

6. The two categories of sexual harassment include:
    a. Quid pro quo and situational
    b. Quid pro quo and hostile environment
    c. Retaliation and hostile environment
    d. Quo dominus and environmental force

7. The boss tells one of her employees that if he spends the night with her, he will get a bonus and a salary increase. This is an example of:
    a. Quid pro quo sexual harassment
    b. Quo dominus sexual harassment
    c. Hostile work environment sexual harassment
    d. Acceptable workplace romance

8. Once a person engages in a sexual relationship with a supervisor, they cannot later claim they were sexually harassed.
    a. True
    b. False

9. In the workplace, Sarah tells Larry an off-color joke with vulgar language that was intended for Larry's ears only. Amelia was within earshot of them, heard the entire joke and was very offended. Has sexual harassment occurred?
    a. No, because the conversation was private between Sarah and Larry.
    b. No, because Amelia would be viewed as eavesdropping on Sarah and Larry.
    c. Yes, because Amelia was exposed to their conversation.
    d. No, because there was no intent for Amelia to be a part of the conversation.

10. Simon heard Jennifer, Rick's boss, offer to give Rick a promotion if he met her at a downtown hotel after work. Based on this, who could file a sexual harassment complaint?
    a. Rick, because this represents quid pro quo sexual harassment.
    b. No one, because nothing has yet occurred.
    c. Simon could file a hostile work environment sexual harassment claim.
    d. a & c

11. Just staring or making suggestive looks can be the basis for a sexual harassment complaint.
    a. True
    b. False

12. Which of the following is an example of third-party sexual harassment?
    a. Being told an off-color joke by a co-worker
    b. Being sexually harassed by a person who has harassed another
    c. Being sexually harassed by a nonemployee over which the company could exercise some control, such as a delivery person
    d. All of the above
    e. None of the above

13. Under third-party sexual harassment, customers must be protected on your property.
    a. True
    b. False

14. A complaint of sexual harassment should be filed with the U.S. Office of Equal Employment Opportunity Commission (EEOC) and/or the state's department of human rights within how many days of the last day of the most recent harassment event?
    a. 365
    b. 90 (180 in some states)
    c. 180 (300 in some states)
    d. 30 (365 in some states)

15. Which of the following is true regarding sexual harassment?
    a. Gender of the accused and the accuser is irrelevant.
    b. Behavior is sexual in nature and unwelcome.
    c. Complainants may file a lawsuit against both the employer and the employee allegedly involved in the sexual harassment.
    d. Due to changes in laws, periodic sexual harassment training is necessary.
    e. All of the above
    f. None of the above

CHAPTER 9

Business Ethics

Businesses with a loyal customer base are also those that consistently behave ethically. Unethical behavior can be confused with illegal behavior. The former isn't necessarily a crime, but it is a great way to lose customers.

Formally defined:
Ethics are the written and unwritten codes of principles and values that govern decisions and actions in terms of rights, obligations and benefits to society, and the ongoing growth of those codes.

More practically defined:
Ethics are the standards of behavior that tell us how human beings ought to act in the many situations in which we find ourselves as friends, parents, children, citizens, businesspeople, professionals, or in other capacities or relationships.

Unethical vs. Illegal Behavior

Let's look at examples of illegal and unethical business behaviors.

EXAMPLE OF ILLEGAL BUSINESS BEHAVIOR

Because of the busy nature of the job and because most customers are of the younger generation, Bob's Bistro actively recruits waitstaff who are under the age of 30.

This example is a clear legal violation of age discrimination in the workplace. Per federal EEOC regulations, it is **unlawful** to discriminate against a person because of their age with respect to any term, condition or privilege of employment—including, but not limited to, hiring, firing, promoting, layoff, compensation, benefits, job assignments and training. An exception is a bona fide occupational qualification. Bona fide occupational qualifications are often used for safety reasons, such as imposing a mandatory retirement age for airline pilots and bus drivers. The business owner is required to provide proof in these instances.

While "Bob" may feel that younger individuals relate more readily to his customer base and perform better in the waitstaff role, automatically excluding anyone over the age of 30 from employment is illegal, and "Bob" may pay dearly in the courts for this behavior.

EXAMPLES OF UNETHICAL BUSINESS BEHAVIOR

Recently, we hired a company to power wash and seal our deck. They sent an individual out to look over our two-level deck and then emailed us an estimate. The price listed on their estimate was much higher than we expected, so we phoned the business owner to share our concerns with him. He looked up our estimate and replied that he had provided us a bid for another job by mistake and then offered a lower cost estimate, which was more what we had expected, so we accepted the bid.

A couple of days later, his crew came to our house and power washed the deck. They indicated they would return to seal the deck in a few days, after the wood had time to dry thoroughly. A couple of days later, the owner called to advise us that materials required to seal the deck would cost $500. When I shared that their estimate clearly stated "labor and materials" were included, he again said that he had looked at someone else's estimate in error. His crew subsequently finished the job and we paid them the amount we had earlier agreed upon.

So, did the owner do anything illegal? Certainly nothing that could be proven as such. Did he do anything unethical? Absolutely! At minimum, the business needed to review its practices and make corrections to reduce the aforementioned "errors." Sadly, for them, we will not be repeat customers.

Not all unethical behavior is as blatant as the above instance. Some examples:

- **Taking office products home.** Many years ago in one of the offices where I worked, I went to the supply cabinet for some adhesive tape. There was another person there, and when I mentioned I could not find any adhesive tape, she stated, "It's Christmastime; there's never any tape left during Christmastime." While taking pens, paper and other items from your workplace may seem innocent enough, it is clearly unethical, and in significant situations may be prosecutable or grounds for disciplinary action or termination.

- **Taking credit for work you didn't do.** During one of my corporate work assignments, we would travel to another city for monthly staff meetings. I was eager to share a special project I had worked on with my boss and co-workers. As we were going around the table presenting information, a co-worker grabbed my project and gave it to the boss, intimating he had completed the work. This was clearly unethical. By the way, I chose to not embarrass the co-worker and said nothing in the large group, but did confront the co-worker later. Our collective supervisor already knew who did the work and appreciated my not making an issue of it in the large meeting.

- **Abrupt schedule changes.** Let's assume you had received approval from your boss six months ago for a vacation to take your family to a major theme park for a week. You purchased airline tickets, booked lodging at the resort, and paid for multi-day park tickets. Just a day or two before your scheduled vacation, your boss tells you that an urgent project must be completed and you need to cancel your vacation. You can imagine the extreme emotion arising—for you and your family. Is this illegal? No, but it certainly falls well within the unethical camp, particularly if this is a repeated behavior.

Behavior that is illegal is prohibited by law and can cause the offender to face profoundly dire consequences. Unethical behavior represents activities not conforming to approved social or professional standards of behavior and can impact the morale of the workplace, which directly affects customer interactions.

Values Driving Ethical Behavior

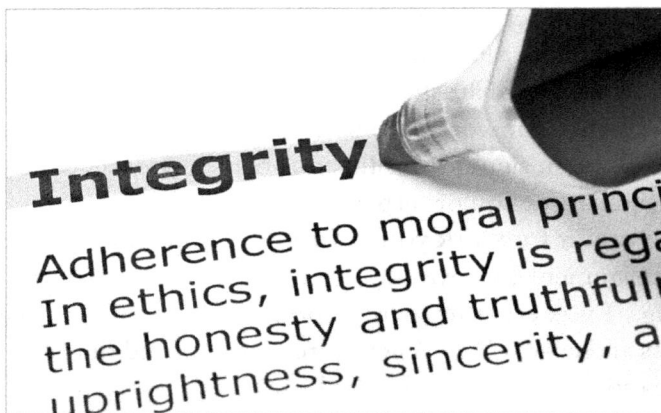

The values that typically drive ethical behavior include, but are not limited to:

- **Integrity.** Making the promises you can keep and keeping the promises you make. Adhering to this principle contributes to positive relationships and higher levels of customer satisfaction.
- **Honesty.** Being truthful—sharing facts with customers and others. Providing factual information—as complete as possible—to your customers allows them to make better, more-informed decisions regarding your organization's products and services.
- **Faithfulness.** Being consistent in your actions toward others and yourself. When you are steadfast in your behaviors to customers and others, you gain their trust and loyalty.
- **Compassion.** Having concern for others—acknowledging their condition. Recognizing and responding to their needs with genuine concern builds lasting relationships.
- **Respect.** Treating others in a manner that makes them feel good. Focusing 100 percent of your attention on the person you are serving at that moment lets them know they are important to you. Being respectable and respectful are the critical pre-cursors to receiving respect.

- **Dignity.** Having positive esteem and bringing that out in others. In all interactions, you must ensure that no one is or may feel devalued in any manner. Remember that everyone has different life experiences; your understanding and patience—appreciating these differences—contributes to overall feelings of being valued.

Ethics is knowing the difference between what you have a right to do and what is right to do.

—POTTER STEWART

Reporting Unethical Behavior

There is trivial difference between observing unethical behavior in the workplace then doing nothing and directly engaging in unethical behavior. Ignoring unethical behavior can have significant consequences on the business and its employees.

So, what should you do if you observe unethical behavior?

- First and foremost, ensure you understand the correct procedures for reporting. They are often documented in the company's human resources policy manual.
- Do not report the behavior unless you are sure about the facts. Do not make unsupported accusations under any circumstances. It is risky to take something you heard or observed out of context and draw potentially inaccurate conclusions about unethical behavior.
- Do not "grandstand" the situation—this isn't about you as the "hero"—it is about doing what is right.
- When you are reporting unethical behavior, it is important to:
  ○ Be impartial.
  ○ State what happened—using factual statements only.

- ° Clarify what you consider unethical about the situation and why.
- ° Identify any employer liability that may result from this behavior.
- ° Maintain appropriate confidentiality. Again, this isn't about you but what is right.
- Finally, if you are reticent to report such behavior because you fear retaliation, you may be entitled to "whistleblower" protection. Whistleblower protection laws and regulations guarantee freedom of speech for workers and contractors in certain situations. If in doubt, check with an attorney, as regulations may vary based on circumstances, location and authority.

Practicing Ethical Behavior

Every day you can double-check your own ethical practices by asking yourself some simple questions:
- Did I live my values today?
- Did I do good while ensuring not to do any harm today?
- Did I treat everyone with dignity and respect today, even though some interactions might have been challenging?
- Was I fair to everyone today?
- Were my organization and I both better because I was a part of it?

Remember, customers are attracted, and remain loyal, to enterprises that consistently behave honestly and with integrity. Do what you say you will do, even when no one is watching, and your customers will reward you.

Chapter Review Questions

1. A practical definition of ethical behavior could include, "Standards of behavior that tell us how human beings ought to act in many situations."
   a. True
   b. False

2. Tyree's Appliance Repair regularly does not return calls to customers. This behavior:
   a. Is illegal activity in the majority of states
   b. Can be cause for serious criminal charges
   c. Is not illegal
   d. Is a federal crime under the FCC because it involves telephone communication

3. Which of the following is not illegal behavior?
   a. Selecting employees based on age
   b. Giving employment preference to a close relative
   c. Avoiding hiring a person you believe to be overweight
   d. Refusing service to a customer based on unusual religious practices

4. Unethical behavior represents activities not conforming to approved social or professional standards of behavior.
   a. True
   b. False

5. Which of the following is not a value associated with ethical behavior?
   a. Situationality
   b. Honesty
   c. Respect
   d. Integrity

6. Why might some companies unfortunately not provide ethics training to employees?
   a. It is a "soft" versus "hard" skill.
   b. It is considered common sense.
   c. Employees already know employer expectations.
   d. All of the above
   e. None of the above

7. Which of the following is a good reason for providing employees training in ethics?
   a. Clarifies expectations for employees in challenging situations
   b. Provides employees solid reasons to behave more appropriately with others
   c. Reinforces that the organization does not approve of unethical behavior
   d. All of the above
   e. None of the above

8. Observing unethical behavior and not reporting it is much different than actually engaging in unethical behavior.
   a. True
   b. False

9. Which of the following should you not do if you observe unethical behavior?
    a. Ensure you know the facts.
    b. Take sides as appropriate.
    c. Maintain proper confidentiality.
    d. Clarify what you consider to be unethical and why.

10. Individuals who observe unethical behavior may be eligible for
"whistleblower" protection.
    a. True
    b. False

11. Which of the following is not an example of unethical behavior?
    a. Taking credit for another's work
    b. Taking minor office products home
    c. Returning a customer's call the next day
    d. Chronic last-minute schedule changes

12. Which of the following would contribute to ethical behaviors?
    a. Living your values daily
    b. Striving to do no harm
    c. Treating everyone with dignity and respect
    d. Being fair to everyone
    e. All of the above
    f. None of the above

CHAPTER 10

Workplace Safety

Maintaining a workplace that is safe for all customers, visitors and employees is extremely important. If your organization does not have a policy or procedure dealing with safety in your place of business, we encourage you to advance discussion with your supervisor or manager to proactively document appropriate actions to be taken to ensure safety for all.

Put yourself in the following situation, which my wife, youngest (adult) daughter and I experienced on January 13, 2018, while vacationing in West Maui, Hawaii. That morning, my wife and I decided to drive a short distance to a favorite eatery for breakfast. Just as we pulled into the parking lot, both of our cell phones started buzzing continuously. When we accessed our phones, we both received the following emergency broadcast alert:

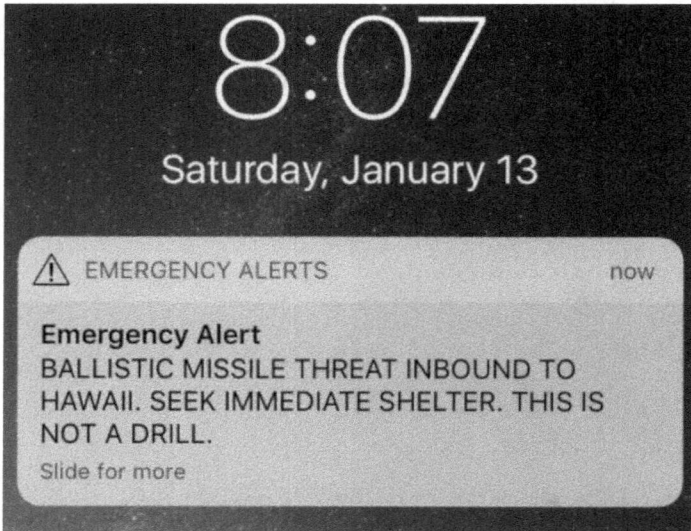

8:07

Saturday, January 13

⚠ EMERGENCY ALERTS   now

Emergency Alert
BALLISTIC MISSILE THREAT INBOUND TO
HAWAII. SEEK IMMEDIATE SHELTER. THIS IS
NOT A DRILL.
Slide for more

Now, living in the Midwest, we have encountered numerous thunder-storm and tornado warnings. This, though, was in a class of its own, to say the least.

We rushed back to our resort—my wife to our condo to be with our daughter, while I went to the front desk, where there were many other resort guests all asking the same question: "What should we do? What safety measures can we take?" The reply we received was, "They haven't told us what to do in this kind of situation." And they offered nothing further. We quickly interpreted this response to suggest that "you are on your own!"

We both immediately got on our laptops to see what we could find about the "incoming ballistic missile." Part of us wanted to believe it was a mistake. Another part was horrified that we only had 23 minutes (or less) to live. Should we call our other daughter and grandchildren to say goodbye?

Approximately 35–40 minutes later we received an emergency bulletin that the earlier warning was a mistake and there was, in fact, no inbound ballistic missile. The official report later indicated that "Someone clicked the wrong **thing** on the computer."

Interestingly enough, we did not panic and instead remained calm during this ordeal. Reflectively, we were surprised by the resort's lack of emergency preparedness. While an incoming ballistic missile would unlikely ever be on a business's safety training curriculum, some kind of response from the resort representative about the safest options for us would have been comforting.

Why share this anecdote? Because most of you at one time or another have faced an emergency situation where action is required by you that falls outside the scope of your normal daily duties. It is incumbent on you and your organization to have proactively planned a mitigating course of action to the extent possible and practical for the more likely situations.

Let's look at three important areas of workplace safety that may require your special attention as a Customer Service Professional.

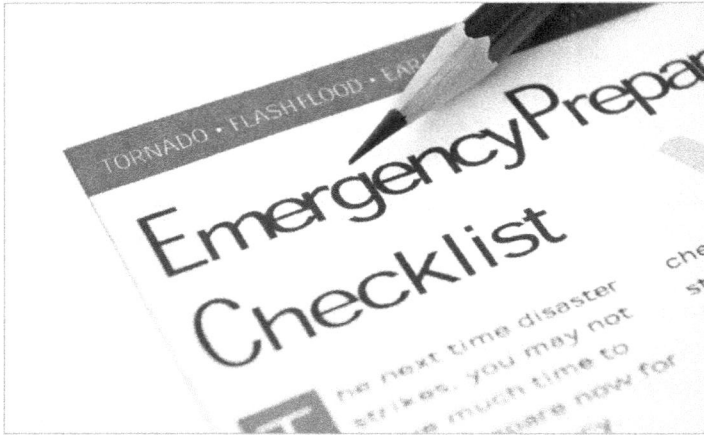

Weather Issues and Considerations

A significant component of workplace safety involves weather changes that may compromise the well-being of people and facilities. Depending on your geographical region, various weather-related concerns may apply. These include:

- **Flooding.** Flooding is the most common environmental disaster in the United States. It can occur anywhere and anytime there is a temporary overflow of water on land that is usually dry. It is, unfortunately, a serious cause of injury and death.
- **Tornadoes.** Tornadoes can happen anywhere and anytime that weather is conducive for such events. However, the Midwest and Southeast regions of the United States have an elevated risk of experiencing a tornado. Tornadoes can be quite deadly—with winds sometimes exceeding 200 miles per hour.
- **Thunderstorms.** These storms can be damaging and deadly. Thunder is the result of lightning. And the primary cause of injury or death in a thunderstorm is from lightning. Though most people survive a direct lightning strike, they may experience

longer-term incapacitating issues. Hail may accompany a thunderstorm and cause significant property damage as well as injury to individuals—sometimes death.

- **Hurricanes.** Hurricanes are extremely dangerous and can occur anywhere along the United States coastline. They typically cause severe damage due to high wind and flooding as well as deaths linked directly to the actual storm surge or subsequent violent storms.

- **Earthquakes.** Earthquakes occur without notice. Obviously, the stronger the earthquake, the greater the destruction and, often, loss of life. Like tornadoes, earthquakes can occur anywhere; however, in the United States they more often occur in Hawaii, California, Alaska, Washington, Oregon and the entire Mississippi River Valley—including all or part of 13 states in the mid-central United States.

It is important that in any of these potential weather emergencies, we are prepared to provide as much safety and security as possible to co-workers and customers. Businesses must have emergency instructions immediately available when a weather-related event is imminent or likely to occur. Ensure you understand clearly when and where to take shelter.

Following is an excellent example of the value of weather-related emergency preparedness:

Tornado warnings were being broadcast for Central Illinois on Tuesday, July 13, 2004. At 2:41 p.m., a fabrication company became the target of a direct hit from the full force of an F4-class tornado—with winds exceeding 240 miles per hour. The manufacturing buildings—over 250,000 square feet—were totally destroyed. Debris was scattered for several miles.

What about the company's 150 employees, many of whom were in the building at the time of the tornado? All survived; none were injured. How is this possible? Two factors are credited for this miracle, if you will.

1. The company had three hardened storm shelters in which all employees took refuge.
2. The company planned and practiced a severe weather emergency procedure.

Before this event, it was rumored that many employees felt the tornado drills were excessive. Obviously, that sentiment changed rather quickly.

This example truly drives home the need to understand what could occur in your region and implement a plan to be prepared. Taking proactive steps may contribute to reducing injuries and saving lives.

When the ambulance shows up, it's a bit late to plan for what may be inside!

—C. William Crutcher

Medical Emergencies

As a Customer Service Professional, you may encounter a customer needing some form of medical attention. While most of us are not trained to handle more complicated medical issues, there are some medical situations for which we could be prepared.

What is a medical emergency in the workplace? It can be defined as a sudden illness, injury or condition serious enough to require immediate medical attention. Because these situations occur unexpectedly, they can be alarming. This is especially true if you or your company find yourselves unprepared for such crises. We can be better prepared to address these situations by learning reasonable measures to implement when facing a medical emergency. The goal is to minimize injuries and, in extreme situations, save a life.

Understandably, instructing readers on actual steps to take in case of a medical emergency is beyond the scope of this writing. Being familiar

146

with first aid AED (automated external defibrillator) location and use—if available—and CPR (cardiopulmonary resuscitation) can help you prevent or minimize serious injury. It can even save lives. Knowing what to do can give you the confidence to act calmly and quickly.

You can find additional information on first aid, AED and CPR courses through the **Red Cross** and the **National CPR Foundation.** Availability of training may vary depending on location.

Workplace Violence

A word of caution: This information is provided to inform the Customer Service Professional regarding violence in the workplace. **It is not intended, nor should it be viewed, as a substitute for your company's policies, procedures and instructions** on handling workplace safety issues. Readers must not feel equipped to engage in workplace safety intervention in any manner by means of the information herein shared.

So, what is workplace violence? Workplace violence is defined as any act or threat of physical violence, harassment, intimidation or other threatening behavior that occurs at the employee's work site. It ranges from threats and verbal abuse to physical assaults and even homicide. It can adversely impact employees, clients, customers and visitors.

While threatening behavior can occur in face-to-face, telephonic and virtual settings, it is especially important to consider the safety of customers and others in your **immediate physical presence.**

VIOLENT OR THREATENING BEHAVIOR
Extreme behavior can be categorized by its increasing level of intensity.
- **Verbal abuse.** Includes insults of protected classes under Title VII of the Civil Rights Act of 1964 and subsequent amendments, name-calling, or any other kind of verbal abuse directed at, witnessed or overheard by another person, whether that person is a co-worker, supervisor, customer, supplier or visitor.

- **Indirect threats.** Includes statements such as "You're going to be sorry you did that to me," or "Bosses who do things like that should be killed." These threats may be indirect, but they are still unacceptable.
- **Direct threats.** Here, the threats are clearly aimed at a particular person, and stipulate a specific action. This type of violent behavior includes intimidation and statements such as "I'll break your arm next time," or "I'll kill you."
- **Nonverbal threats.** Actions such as hitting motions—even if no actual contact is made—or obscene gestures also qualify as violent behavior that will not be tolerated.
- **Extreme threats.** Includes stalking or forcing unwanted attention on someone, whether romantic or hostile. Another form of extreme threat is displaying a gun, knife, or anything that could be perceived as a weapon.
- **Violent actions.** Actual physical violence. Violent acts that in any way are likely to cause bodily harm or property damage are clearly not to be tolerated.

STAGES OF VIOLENCE

In addition to recognizing warning signs of violence, understanding the phases of violent behavior is also important. Psychologists and other experts in workplace violence generally recognize three stages of violent behavior.

- **Level 1—Initial potential for violence.** The first level involves treating other people as objects or debasing them. This includes name-calling and other insults or offensive language. It might also include questioning authority and insubordination as well as being consistently confrontational and alienating customers or co-workers.
- **Level 2—Increased potential for violence.** In level 2 the behavior becomes more overt. The individual may start ignoring company policies and procedures, stealing from the company or co-workers, blaming others for problems, damaging property, or making threats orally, in writing, by email or voicemail.

- **Level 3—Potential for violence carried out.** Level 3 denotes open violent behavior—displaying or flaunting a gun, knife, explosive device, or other weapon or device that could be a weapon; hitting, kicking or slapping a victim; committing a physical attack; or setting a fire. In this phase, we would also include attempted suicide, as an employee attempting to hurt themselves is considered workplace violence.

Again, knowing the levels of workplace violence progression and how they can evolve—often very quickly—is important for direct-contact Customer Service Professionals to fully understand, along with your organization's workplace safety policies and procedures.

GENERAL SECURITY MEASURES

Following are some actions that can minimize violent behavior in the workplace:

- Understand and follow your company's policies regarding visitors. They may include requiring visitors to sign in at the reception desk, wear visible visitors' badges, or be escorted within the facility.
- Know the name and phone number of the people to whom you report a potential workplace safety issue (for example, burned out lighting or unescorted strangers).
- There are many security measures that can minimize the threat of violence from outside the company. For example:
  - **Keep security doors closed and locked.** This may seem like an obvious precaution, but take a look around. Are there any doors that are inappropriately propped open or left carelessly unlatched at your facility?
  - **Do not share ID cards or security codes with others.** This applies regardless of the circumstances or the apparent trustworthiness of nonemployees.

- ° **Follow rules for visitors.** These rules not only protect employees but they also protect visitors from potential workplace hazards.
- ° **Report unescorted strangers.** Strangers observed within the facility should be reported immediately. A person without a known business purpose should not be allowed access to nonpublic areas of the workplace.
- ° **Report damaged or insufficient lighting.** Poor lighting can provide the kind of environment that criminals—anyone with violent intentions—can use to their advantage. It can also allow for unnecessary slips and falls, which is a workplace safety issue as well.
- ° **Report unusual or unexpected deliveries.** Do not allow unusual or unexpected deliveries to be opened until their contents can be determined. Such packages could contain something hazardous.
- ° **Report any signs of break-ins or missing items.** Any signs of unauthorized entry and any thefts should be reported and investigated.
- ° **Take appropriate precautions when working late.** Let someone know where you are in the building after hours, lock the door to the work area if you're alone and use caution leaving the building and walking to your vehicle or transportation. Having an escort—especially after dark—is advisable in these situations.

Again, you are not expected to, nor should you ever, **without proper training and approval,** attempt to confront violent workplace situations. By remaining observant and cautious, everyone can contribute to a safer work environment for themselves, fellow employees, visitors and customers. Operate from the principle that workplace safety is everyone's job.

Chapter Review Questions

1. Which of the following is not a workplace safety issue?
   a. Flooding
   b. Threat of incoming ballistic missile
   c. Violent customer
   d. Co-worker requiring CPR
   e. None of the above

2. Flooding is the most common environmental disaster in the United States.
   a. True
   b. False

3. Which of following is true about hurricanes?
   a. They can occur anywhere along the United States coastline.
   b. They cause severe damage due to high winds.
   c. Hurricane deaths are typically related to the storm surge.
   d. Flooding is associated with them.
   e. All of the above
   f. None of the above

4. If your organization does not have policies and procedures for dealing with workplace emergencies, there is little you can do.
   a. True
   b. False

5. Where are the best places to receive CPR training?
   a. From a co-worker
   b. The Red Cross
   c. National CPR Foundation
   d. All of the above
   e. b & c

6. You should receive proper training in dealing with workplace medical emergencies to reduce the likelihood of doing further harm.
   a. True
   b. False

7. Which of the following is true regarding workplace safety?
   a. Do not intervene in a workplace violence situation unless specifically trained to do so.
   b. Follow your organization's policies, procedures and instructions for handling a workplace safety issue.
   c. Workplace violence can involve employees, clients, customers and visitors.
   d. Threatening behavior can occur in face-to-face, telephonic and virtual settings.
   e. All of the above

8. Indirect threats can typically be ignored as they do not result in subsequent violent action.
   a. True
   b. False

9. Which of the following represents violent or threatening behavior?
   a. Verbal abuse
   b. Indirect threats
   c. Nonverbal threats
   d. Violent actions
   e. All of the above

10. In a "level 3" stage of violence, which of the following is not likely to occur?
    a. Open violent behavior
    b. Name-calling
    c. Display of a gun, knife, explosive device or anything being used or threatened as a weapon
    d. Kicking or slapping a victim

11. Harm to self is included in level 3 violence.
    a. True
    b. False

12. The visitor policy at Tim's company may include the following common requirements for visitors:
    a. Must sign in at reception desk
    b. Must wear visible visitor badge
    c. Must be escorted within the facility
    d. Must be fingerprinted upon entry to the facility
    e. All of the above
    f. a, b & c

13. Burned-out lighting does not represent a problem relative to workplace safety.
    a. True
    b. False

14. Which of the following can contribute to enhanced workplace safety?
    a. Reporting unusual or unexpected deliveries
    b. Being escorted to your car when working late and after dark
    c. Keeping unattended doors closed and locked
    d. Reporting signs of break-in or missing items
    e. All of the above
    f. None of the above

15. We should never, without proper training and approval, confront violent workplace situations.
    a. True
    b. False

Chapter Review Questions: Answer Grid

Chapter 1: Foundations of Customer Service

1. b
2. b
3. e
4. b
5. a
6. d
7. a
8. b
9. a
10. d
11. b
12. b
13. b
14. b
15. e

Chapter 2: Building Customer Relationships

1. b
2. d
3. b
4. c
5. a
6. a
7. a
8. a
9. b
10. c
11. b
12. a

13.   a
14.   c
15.   e

Chapter 3: Insight into Customer Behavior

1.   d
2.   b
3.   d
4.   b
5.   b
6.   a
7.   b
8.   b
9.   a
10.   a
11.   b
12.   d
13.   a
14.   b
15.   e
16.   a
17.   a
18.   c
19.   b
20.   d
21.   a

Chapter 4: Engaging in Successful Communication

1.   b
2.   a
3.   b
4.   d
5.   b

6.   b
7.   c
8.   a
9.   b
10.   b
11.   e
12.   a
13.   d
14.   c
15.   b
16.   a

Chapter 5: Customer Interaction

1.   b
2.   a
3.   c
4.   d
5.   a
6.   e
7.   b
8.   a
9.   e
10.   c
11.   b
12.   e
13.   b
14.   b
15.   c
16.   e
17.   a
18.   b
19.   c
20.   b

Chapter 6: Effective Email Communication

1. c
2. b
3. d
4. b
5. d
6. a
7. c
8. a
9. b
10. a
11. e
12. a
13. e
14. b
15. f
16. b

Chapter 7: Appreciating the Impact of Stress

1. b
2. a
3. a
4. b
5. e
6. a
7. c
8. e
9. a
10. b
11. b
12. e
13. b
14. d

15.   a

Chapter 8: Sexual Harassment—Principles and Prevention

1.   c
2.   b
3.   a
4.   a
5.   d
6.   b
7.   a
8.   b
9.   c
10.   d
11.   a
12.   c
13.   a
14.   c
15.   e

Chapter 9: Business Ethics

1.   a
2.   c
3.   b
4.   a
5.   a
6.   d
7.   d
8.   b
9.   b
10.   a
11.   c
12.   e

Chapter 10: Workplace Safety

1.   e
2.   a
3.   e
4.   b
5.   e
6.   a
7.   e
8.   b
9.   e
10.   b
11.   a
12.   f
13.   b
14.   e
15.   a

Acknowledgments

First, and foremost, I am thankful for my life partner of many years, Diane Crutcher. Her professional expertise and collaboration have been critical in the development of the comprehensive education and training programs at the National Customer Service Association. Her ongoing personal support has inspired me to develop this book. Because of her, this publication moved well beyond just a concept and some hopeful thinking.

I want to recognize the thousands and thousands of frontline Customer Service Professionals I have encountered over the years. These encounters have contributed significantly to my understanding of what really defines both positive and not-so-positive customer experiences.

Thank you to the thousands of researchers and writers that continue to recognize that excellent customer service is essential for every organization. All play an important role in advancing this critical field.

Following are special people who have inspired my ongoing learning and, in doing so, have certainly contributed to this book.

- Wes Tindal, current president of the NCSA Central Florida Chapter and chief operating officer of the National Customer Service Association. His passion for service is incomparable.
- Nivi Nagiel. Such a knowledgeable, skilled editor and an important partner in this process. Your comprehension of the written word is amazing.
- Pam Germer. Her intuitive approach to design causes words to come to life. For many years, she has been and remains an integral part of our team.
- Always must include Henry Ford. "Yes, I think I can!"
- All current and former members of the military who exemplify service. I salute you always!
- Amie and Mindie. You both are my heroes. In the face of adversity, you both excel. We need to find a way to bottle your determination and give it to others.

161

About the Author

C. William (Bill) Crutcher is president and CEO of the National Customer Service Association (NCSA). Crutcher began his business career after completing a tour of duty as a U.S. Army sergeant in the northern Quang Tri Province of South Vietnam. His military duties prepared him well for the physical, intellectual and emotional challenges he would face after military life.

Crutcher held numerous managerial and leadership roles in the fields of engineering, security and finance in the telephony industry for nearly 30 years. During this period, he traveled the country, speaking at numerous finance conferences. He is also a Life-Certified Treasury Professional.

Crutcher obtained a Bachelor of Business Administration degree and an MBA from Illinois State University—both earned through night school while juggling full-time work and family opportunities. It was during this time that Crutcher developed his attraction to the discipline of human dynamics. This led him to become an adjunct college professor in management and organizational behavior following his corporate career. He then began exploring new ways of thinking about decision-making trends and challenged himself to think differently about the then tried-and-true approaches. To that end, he created many proprietary managerial models and approaches focusing on a variety of topics, including:

- Employee performance
- Strategic planning
- Customer service strategies

- Change management
- Business development
- Project management

Garnering extensive knowledge through his work with organizations of all sizes—private and public—as well as his work with thousands of adult students, in both the Center for Performance Development, Inc., and the National Customer Service Association, Crutcher became equally effective in roles ranging from executive coach to transforming groups into highly successful teams. He has been highly active in the field of adult education since 1996. Crutcher's considerable expertise in both organizational planning and human dynamics allows him to guide businesses in achieving competitive advantage through the development of customer-centric work cultures.

Crutcher is married and has two adult daughters and two grandchildren. His younger daughter has Down syndrome, and he and his wife co-founded the Central Illinois Down Syndrome Organization (CIDSO) more than 48 years ago. This organization flourishes today and provides educational and support services to individuals touched by Down syndrome in the Central Illinois area. Crutcher continues to donate a considerable amount of his discretionary time to enhancing services for people with cognitive impairments as well as advocating for services for veterans.

www.ingramcontent.com/pod-product-compliance
Lightning Source LLC
Chambersburg PA
CBHW071608210326
41597CB00019B/3454